THE DAUGHTERS

BY STEPHEN BERG

Bearing Weapons
Naked Poetry, co-editor
The Queen's Triangle

THE DAUGHTERS
poems by STEPHEN BERG

THE BOBBS-MERRILL COMPANY, INC.

Indianapolis and New York

TO MY FAMILY

ACKNOWLEDGMENTS

"Everywhere," "Shoes," "Sleep," and "Crutches" were initially published in *Cafe Solo*. Copyright © 1970 by the Solo Press.

"The Queen's Triangle" is reprinted from *The Queen's Triangle* by permission of The Cummington Press, West Branch, Iowa. Copyright © 1970 by Stephen Berg.

"Above All Cattle," "Gooseberries," and "The Return of Black Shag" originally appeared in *December*. Copyright © 1970 by C. L. Johnson.

"Predict? Ask yourself why? Nibble a cheese sandwich? Know?" was first printed in *Inside Outer Space,* edited by Robert Vas Dias. Copyright © 1970 by Doubleday & Company, Inc.

"Good" and "May 1970" were originally published in *The Iowa Review*. Copyright © 1970 by the University of Iowa.

"Rising without names today" (originally entitled "The Survivor"), "People Trying to Love," and "A Late Night Conversation" were initially printed in *New American Review #3*. Copyright © 1968 by the New American Library, Inc.

"Uncle Will, The Gardener" (1964); "To My Friends" and "A Wife Talks to Herself" (1965); "Between Us" (1967); "Suddenly I remember the holes" (originally entitled "The Holes") and "Dreaming with a Friend" (1969) copyrighted ©, in the respective years shown, by the New Yorker Magazine, Inc.

"Eloise Simpson Visits the East," "Who's Next," and "A Glimpse of the Body Shop" are reprinted with permission from *The North American Review*. Copyright © 1968, 1970 by the University of Northern Iowa.

ACKNOWLEDGMENTS

"And So On" (1965); "Going Upstairs to Bed" and "Ollie, Answer Me" (1966); "It'll be much easier when the dead" (originally entitled "The Dead"), "They can tell me the soul rises to its perch" (originally entitled "The Soul"), "Unnamed Shapes," "As the Days Pass and Darken," "Heartache," "The Kiss," "Nick's Photograph of Jeff, Me, and Arlene," "Directions for Being Jesus," and "Times" (1970) first appeared in *Poetry*, and were copyrighted ©, in the respective years indicated, by the Modern Poetry Association.

In the fourth-from-the-last section of "Dark lords who wait until the children exhaust themselves," the last five lines are from "Something on the Death of the Oldest Sabines" by Jaime Sabines. The translation of the five lines is from an adapted version by Philip Levine and is used here with his permission.

"Milk" and "In the Middle" were originally printed in *The Seneca Review*. Copyright © 1970 by *The Seneca Review*.

"Desnos Reading the Palms of Men on Their Way to the Gas Chambers" is reprinted from *Sumac*. Copyright © 1970 by the editors of *Sumac*. Of the final seven lines of the poem, the first three are taken from "La Voix de Robert Desnos" and the last four from "La Voix"; the two poems are from *Domaine Public* by Robert Desnos, copyright © 1953 by Editions Gallimard. The translations of the two excerpts are by William Kulik.

"I'm a pig, I'm a seagull" (originally entitled "The Animals") and sections 3, 11, 15, and 16 of "In the Monument Works" first appeared in *TriQuarterly*. Copyright © 1969 by Northwestern University Press.

"Sister Ann" was originally printed in *TransPacific*. Copyright © 1968 by Nicholas Crome.

CONTENTS

THREE

FOUR

FIVE

THE DAUGHTERS

ONE

ENTERING THE BODY

"We exist."
My face rains on your breast
and lies there, my left hand follows
your mouth, my mouth drinks at the surface
of a dark lip, my legs drift backwards,
my right hand touches nothing.
There is a night when rain falls
from the hard sky of rooms,
when you pull your clothes off
and step forward with hands like the choices
of stone, or like the short closed lawns
of citizens who sleep through the day.
The moon hangs behind one eye,
the streets echo like the depths of old clocks,
the doors sigh inwardly without pleasure,
people rush back and forth between two bodies,
everyone is poor.
On either side of the warmth of our faces
whose life will it be?
Walls freeze behind everyone, hinges
say what you forgot to say,
chairs go on receiving strange bodies,
and you have that same dream
about fathers, about salvation,
like a window being pulled down, like
the grass body, steaming.

It'll be much easier when the dead
lash us with wings,
rise with an ocean of dirt in their mouths
and the slow birth of hair and fingernails.
This afternoon I thought about us,
sleeping in blankets, being fatal,
and it seemed wrong to be on one side.
Thinking about parents and friends dying,
I want loss to be
the one candle in church,
the church to be my spine,
the wax God spills
on my hands daily
to drown us.
But the dead earn a new kind of money,
they shoulder tiny brown coins,
they ride the scorched breath
of telegraph wires into
the silence.
I have resurrected everyone at least once.
I have hidden from the body's cradle.
I have known I was barely possible
and smashed my fingers into the keys.
This afternoon I was ashamed to love us.

6

Rising without names today
I want to be a fat man in America
and carry a gun,
I want to sit for the rest of my life
looking at the walls, collecting,
thinking about those miserable images
of dissection I burst
out of my mother with, dripping.
If my face melts off like wax,
if I am beaten across the thighs
until they stick together,
if I find myself drunk in a strange town
looking for a stranger to be my friend,
if I wake with the sea in my mouth
and the wrong father,
if they take one piece of me each year—
the lobe, the glans, the lid, the cap,
the pit—
I would still want to be as fat
as an elephant, and rule, and demand
all others fall to their knees
and serve me.
Rising without names
or wonder in this country,
my fists hardened many days
in the last ovens.

Will anyone love me if my dreams
take over and grow,
if I become all the lost images
of infinity men fear?
They whip their legless beasts
across this ricefield and that sky,
trailing the poison that stings forever,
trampling us between one hill and the next
without one sign, one
minute or history.
All that saves me is how I sucked
long daggers of ice from the back of
the ice wagon or pedaled out in the twilight smelling my fielder's glove or
played cripple.
I am the god
whose ocean fits into a shoe, whose lust
buttons a shirt, whose past rides a white horse
in a white field,
who hears "Soon" whispered
whenever he bends
over the breasts of someone he loves,
Yes and No,
as I curl up
and listen to the blood crossing.

8

The man
floating just under the surface
is poking his head through,
his neck is like the granite
on insurance buildings, the tips
of his fingers wriggle up through my skin.
Rivers cutting through the slums of the city,
warehouses where we have stored ourselves
in case we are needed,
why have we painted signs with names on them,
why are we still filling up space?
All my brothers
have been released forever
and stand on the riverbank weeping, refusing,
my brothers wake up inside themselves
and think the long girders and stacks are women
who live forever, where coal,
sulphur and the stiff cries of metal pour in.
But the man has risen, like anyone.
Even the flag on the state house looks the same.
Even the wind goes its way.
Even the river hides nothing.
Even the stranger knows everyone as himself.
He waves invisibly
with his good hand, and we see him
as we see ourselves—
a little mist curls on the water from the breath
of small poisonous fishes,
like words from the man who is all of us.

Suddenly I remember the holes,
suddenly I think of a man with no entrances,
no exits, the closed man, with feelers or claws
so sensitive that he can tell
what rock is, or flesh, water or flame.
Where does everything go when it comes in?
What should I do with the pure speech of cells
where we find ourselves?
The river flies, the dusk crawls into the ground,
the moon has our face backwards,
the streets get up and leave,
the sun recklessly feeds our blood.
We could be crouching on the branch, we could be
gnawing the brown feathers and thighs of a new animal,
we could be plotting under the ice while others dream.
But I want the infinite man who sleeps
in my veins to rise, I want to hear
the thin buzzing that floats out of my chest
like an arm of locusts making terrible decisions.
Sometimes I want to die because of this.

They can tell me the soul rises to its perch,
wing for mouth claw for hand cloud for skin.
They can say "I heard my father's voice last evening
sing like rain poured into a living ear . . ."
They can invent the white book using the black
and beat on the invisible doors beyond behind not here
and push through like the leaves droning.
They can sit with legs crossed in the holy silences
breathing until the universe runs home like a dog,
eternity for Thursday resurrection for Goodbye.
They can put the nakedness of children before war.
They can pray for the suffering whose tongues drown
and apologize and explain and draw me in
whispering "His face holds the star the seed in the brow . . ."
Meanwhile I have heard stones cracking in the eyes
of a teacher, bees entering a lawyer's throat,
the cup's smooth narrow lips trying
to communicate with the housewife's boredom.
Meanwhile the soul prepares entrances for the crow,
exits for the dust, flesh for the heaven of kings.

Predict? Ask yourself why? Nibble a cheese sandwich? Know?
The roots are listening but they can't say anything
and I am kissing my wife in the moonlight
for the ten-thousandth time.
I see old suitcases upstairs
filled with memories and hopes and fun,
I lie back in a cigar-shaped country, a ship
orbiting the shores of cool dust.
When the first man sinks onto the moon
I'm going to unravel my American flag
in the bathroom and plant it in the sink.
I'm going to turn on the hot water until the steam
hides me from galaxies and the poor,
sweating their balls off across the street.
My head is clouded with pain.
The sky is cloudy too.
A beautiful sweltering day in the East
at the beginning of June. And what?
Everywhere shots of the moon.
My life seems to have grown. But what?
Eat lunch? Play tennis? Pick up the phone? Laugh?
The land stretches in all directions to the sky.

Everyone is glad when the doors wheeze open and their feet
skim the last ground.
News from the planet Zelda is rushed back
to no one, to an automatic tape spinning at headquarters,
to the wind dragging its tentacles on the roofs,
sucking up fragments of the message,
trailing them through space until they fade
and become the pure unbreakable code among codes.
I wake from this to my own breath,
to someone beside me, alive and delicate,
frozen by the thought of how we have come here
to stay for a while and leave.
There is always someone getting up in the morning,
terrified for the first time because he exists;
there is always someone leaving someone,
terrified of the emptiness of being here
without the other.
I lift my coffee cup very slowly, as if
the hand and the cup need each other.
The grass on all sides is quiet.
People are soft and love to touch each other.
The elm is patient, the sky chooses
to do one thing all its life.

Once I knew, nothing in the leaf could see me,
nothing in the word could tell me what it was,
and the daughters sleep with one arm thrown out to the infinite,
their wish for sunlight on waves needs no future,
and the daughters pass through all forms in a single day,
their laughter gives us the ancient joy of the Gods,
and the daughters kiss without vengeance, they kiss,
nothing escapes the blessing of their love, nothing hits back,
and the daughters bring home a twig stone or feather cupped in their hands
and save the world with these by pointing to them awed,
and the daughters protect the sacred wisdom of speech,
they say anything with complete faith, and forget it,
and the daughters make war more perfectly than the President,
it begins and ends, it is not waged in secret,
I have read their simple misspelled canticles on a blackboard
amazed as they are at the tininess of a fly's wing, and screamed,
and not known where I was and hugged them and wept—
I want to pray like that, like the daughters always budding,
and the daughters lift food to an enemy's lips if he is hungry,
I see them skip in and out of death without a thought, in ecstasy,
they take and demand and surrender, they go empty—
I wish I knew what love was, I could forgive everything,
and the daughters touch anything and play under the sad wings
of parents, slowly as they grow the dreams begin, less
little and more sprout from their breasts like quills,
the daughters lashed in fire at the gates.

I look up from the bottom,
I am open.
I can hear my mother's wishes snowing on three cities,
I can see my father's prayers divided on two plates
and I can hear the invisible organ of trust
calling with roots and fluids.
In a window across the street
a retired sailor leans out and watches me
with his face in his hands,
in the Spanish grocery on the corner
potatoes as big as baby dogs
rest in their bins,
everyone's car ticks and flashes,
the old Jew irons my shirts in his window.
Some look like milk, some like water
or like the emptiness between thighs.
But it all sounds like water, it all
stands in front of us, laughing.
I have seen us, cold as the blood
of young trees, walk down into the grains
and spaces of silence.
Trapped in our hands
the word God rushing past, wings
under bridges, wings gathering
to take root in our backs.
I have watched and slept like a river
and have not seen it.
When I get home
all the roads have been eaten.

Soldiers keep a few important papers
in a breast pocket.
When a cloud moves, their right hands
slip inside the jacket.
When the wind breaks through leaves,
their left hands jump forward on steel.
The papers.
Something like a belt of gold weights,
something the poet with a green leg wore,
gives them a weird heaviness.
They wear necklaces, they walk
in high-topped shoes,
they curse the darkness of books
and sofas.
We were born terrified of the ocean,
gifted with a mad calm, and,
like our fathers, unprepared,
groping for coffee, buying sandwiches,
sitting down in the middle,
our hands and feet
two piles of paper
like roads going straight down.

He comes
but he can't find us trapped in our mother's eyes,
sucking the twilight,
wailing in the cradle.
He comes, you sink into a hillside.
He comes, you sleep in a plastic rose.
I whistle, empty a glass, wash
one of the long meat knives from dinner.
Thirst comes, loss comes, sky comes
and I have a fantasy God laughs
each time pieces of us are chewed away
and saved for the resurrection
and grafted across our lips.
Voices nuzzle the windows. In the
silence at the end of the last day we hear him
glazing the steps with rain,
jamming wires in the locks, gnawing hinges,
his great tongue in mailslots
babbling "Jesus men help understand see me I . . ."

I'm a pig, I'm a seagull,
I'm the man nature chose to be broken.
These bristles and feathers
could have been thoughts, these wings and hooves
could have been the failures of sleep.
Sometimes I nose under the mud, grunting
about pain and weightlessness,
sometimes I cut the water,
imagining myself fat and motionless.
I'm both of these because of my deaths,
I'm a wing because your eyes beg me,
I'm diving into your birth because it's needed,
I'm sinking into the ground because it helps.
When you follow me over a hill
or along a cold stretch of sand
my soft husks of celery and bread scar your face,
you remember leaving yourself behind,
like the sea, calling
"Give me back! Give me back!"
But it was the thought that spoke,
it was the breath without skin that lifted you,
it was the dream about acts choosing like water,
it was your mouth closed over the words
of the first God,
the spine, the tail, the mercy
of dark clothing and work.

TWO

IN THE MONUMENT WORKS

Immortals become mortals,
mortals become immortals;
they live in each other's death
and die in each other's life.

1

Shoes pointing upward, blackened and cracked like fruit skins,
the walls bulging in places, half
an angel's wing trapped in its journey out of the stone,
a limp canvas apron dusted with chips,
dirt rising, sunlight crawling
over the smooth yellow tool handles, over gloves,
over steel tips, sanders, and the possible
flight of hands passing. The dust, the words, no one
and not a living soul to decipher it
and only eyes that don't care
and a face twisted flat against the window
of the monument works.

2

It is in a dream
that Shapiro helps everyone, rescues
the neighborhood from a raid of Germans,
their eyes
freezing the air in Charlie's Market.
He hisses "You can't do this to people!"
His mouth churns like a grinder,
slows, closes
and he listens to himself
echoing from high shelves
behind cans and cereal boxes, "You can't . . ."
Boots, the wet flash of knives, a pit
filled with the skinny red things.

The one blade Shapiro can't control grows
in the chest of a friend
like the thought of cloth wrinkling
or of steel blackening, of favorite objects
losing themselves to each other
where nothing is itself.

3

Counting the stacks on Camden's jagged shore,
he sees the tall fire of plants dancing in the shallows,
he gives each puff of smoke a human name.
He has sat there before,
feet swinging out over the weedy mud, the garbage,
the river burning, oil fires coughing up ash,
the world spinning away
on the frozen curve of the eye.

4

He looks at the skyline again, without memory,
and it is the same except, in tears, bigger.

Black as the bloodstream of the human body
a barge slides past motionlessly
toward the Atlantic.
A shock to see it inching across,
cutting the water so heavily
that the delicate white cry of passage
greets no one.

Sometimes it is as if we live so slowly
each breath is a prayer,
a beseeching, a dumb furious inner "Take me now!"
Sometimes, chairs, neckties,
pearled tarnished club pins and scratched lighters
are what time is
and how we feel about it, a thing
we slump down into or lose in a gritty pocket
or wear.

5

We, the dooms, your future, the bloody fire
between places, dancers on the corpses of who,
we eat what there is. Are you
sitting at a table? Is there food? Us,
the zero washing itself, bones entering the floor,
leaves zigzagging down through silt, through farms
in the lone face of a mirror.

6

At fifteen I biked 3000 miles
through New England and Nova Scotia
with 40 pounds strapped on the carrier:
a pot, a tin plate, sneakers, fork and knife,
blanket, sleeping bag, books, a first aid kit,
underwear, boots, a scout knife, three white shirts
and a photograph of my parents.

There at this moment, I hold the photograph,
fifty days, the stars packed in tight
over my face, like grain, pine needles mixed
with the waters of a lake, breathing, rustling.
Who is it?
A thickness, streams between skinbanks, hungers,
a series of old motions, grunts, the odor
of rock moss drifting up before sleep . . .

I can still feel the back wheel swaying
under the weight
and two small gray figures holding hands
in my back pocket.

7

For a few days I am held by the canvas bottom
like an old Jew who has not fled God
and soon

I will pass through the cloth
through layers one by one until I am nothing
until I reach the time
where death, stone, and moisture
jump into the dry house of voices.

When we reached the cliff we saw
Halifax smoking like a huge coal, the blue salt
of waves blowing through steel fires,
jacketing the pines. But with stars

I leaned up into the breasts and sucked for five months.
I was rocked and cleaned and dressed by my mother.
These are my toys.
A grandmother, grandfather, gone,
mother, father, insects to burn
and now the nightfall inside fingers
coming to life.
I was angry at linoleum and death. Noises hurt me.
The sky is like the blue linoleum floor
of my bedroom, when I was five, and knew
all things from the inside.

8

There are five roads to joy:

> avoid metal
> forget
> reject dreams
> eat
> fail

9

The truck has unloaded its blue girders, it pushes
West toward Iowa

where the land, naked and soft, sticks up everywhere
in stalks, in the broken grass of possessions
and riverbeds.
                    Cheticamp, Grand Etang, Pleasant Bay
and Ingonish—the drive steers our truck over a
drop of two thousand feet into the gulf.
Under clouds breaking, under the chant of tires
and the names of a strange world
I continue to fill my hands in streets you just miss—

little places where trees outnumber the men,
enemies, porchlights thick as lightning bugs, rakes,
pale woodslat houses flickering, whiskey,
the twin forms hiding, the unconscious miserable hunger, this

and the mysterious white lines unread forever
this and the miraculous life in the flesh beforehand
this and the breast without memory

10

The need is great
until it burns, until the lids sting with vision
until the woman beside us in bed
or in a cold field on stubble
or on a table with her legs hanging
is waking

I call her each night
and beg her to meet me in the tennis court
where we can show each other
the thin inward cry of the human skull desiring,
a hand sliding downward,
the breath of grasses after cutting time lost in our blood.

11

Mexico City has a darkness like
the moon bleaching the eternal snow of the peaks
on all sides, or like
the booths in The Thresher Diner on The Amazon
where Hitler, Roosevelt, and Mussolini
eat their meals. Candles, flies, plans.

At Temple, the classroom walls have red stains
where one teacher lost his head when he began to think
where a blind student believed it was rain
where a girl tripped, and someone's mind was steady.

O Lord, we married and packed the car
and drove South
into the groin of America
over the hard green plains
hugging the fencewire
through Louisiana's wild sugarcane, lightless
where the gods decided not to have a history
where invisible zebra sang to each other
where sullen fires glowed across the Atlantic
to this shore.

Cattle at the gates of hell,
500 miles of cactus and sky before the orange groves
and the drunk Korean veteran's hotel
in Paradise,
before we could drink again.

Five years later
we still have an orange from there.
It is all spirit now, having slowly

reversed itself into a globe
as light and dry as the skull of a dead hawk
or the silences

but it's written that a man and not a man
saw and saw not a bird and not a bird
high in a tree and no tree and struck it
and struck not with a stone and not a stone

12

Is the shit-colored man God?

On the other shore, in the autopsy room
overlooking the university, two green corpses
hold their stiff nameless grins
in response to nothing, a toe
someone forgot to sew back on
trapped by itself in a corner of the tin pan
they lie in. They are stitched like handmade dolls,
benign and powerless as old genitals
that hang off to one side.

13

Spelling the name of a new country,
the letters glow like tall silver code
riveted to the bridge,
making loose weird fish shapes in the river,
a blue furnace of whales, a jelly
sending up flesh from the city
of bones and beer cans.
A moon smiles thinly under its veil,
a dull green mist.
Suddenly, beyond moneychangers and streetlights

in the border town,
on the desert fanning away into the distance
at red hills,
stars break out over us in slow explosions,
the night deepens.

14

In the city where Sam, Rick's piano player,
plays in a bar,
I worked as a chauffeur
for a famous playboy millionaire builder who was
escaping from barracks that had collapsed,
from hangars weak as cardboard,
wiring from bathrooms for money from Swiss banks,
drinking two bottles of gin a day, screwing his maids,
bribing officials so he could build an oceanfront hotel
that would never be finished.
                        Carrier of Zsa Zsa's
black pearl cufflinks, bringer of synthetic hormones,
of blue baby combs and wheat germ and long needles,
messenger of the abolition of death and kindness,
hider of unmarked vials,
smuggler of a man's fate from L.A. to Acapulco,
librarian of steel, concrete, and the laws of stress,
I can hear time go by again in the two hour nightly sleep
of a dead man,
of a skeleton drawing out three million dollar bank checks,
hiring a full-time pimp,
hiring everyone in sight so he could see himself in the mirror.

In my mind I kept driving us off a cliff,
in my mind I wanted three floors overlooking the Pacific,
in my mind I wanted his calm golf club in the mountains,
in my mind I wanted the silence of the presidential mouths

on all that cash,
in my mind I wanted his greatest invention,
one sentence in perfect American—
"Money is God in Circulation."

His words stand like one of those giant redwoods
with a door through it.

15

In a horse's guts pecked out
by vultures on the road to Oaxaca,
in a ragged chunk of artery
I saw the Four Edges:

> The horse was dead
> The horse was alive
> The horse wasn't dead or alive
> The horse

The arrows of
The Lacandon Indians
have barbs
all along the shaft
so a monkey
hit in the belly
will tear himself to pieces when
he pulls it out.

The wives walk behind
their men
fixing a stray tassel
carrying the money
admiring the most beautiful
male legs in the world
keeping these representatives

of God
in shape for the fire.

When Jim, Lou, Jeff and I
swallowed the white crystals
the world blew into a flame,
we cried
at the miracle
of the look of hands.

16

Now the veined hands of both my fathers
let me go into
the twilight of comic books. Secret
folded notes stuffed in a cigar box
strung between windows over the alley
between our houses
fall again.
I see her triangle, soft and hairless as a cloud,
gleaming under the night light,
Teddy's fingers twisting away from his unknown cancer,
hands dropping tiny newts, stones being heated,
the baseball field, stubbly
friends

smoke twirls up
through a little hole
in the roof
the mules try each rock
before stepping down
into the village with
loads of branches
that cover them
thick and green, the valley
smolders and is

penetrated only
by those who can suffer
the heat
and the isolation of
placeless birth
I follow the shaggy strings
blowing apart
the dung everywhere
clubbing our nostrils
nothing for me
except to live here

we drove away
from that slow world, those people
of the skin of evening
eaters of all flesh
friends

17

Many old trees line the streets of this city
and you can touch them.
Many of us have touched each other
and that is proof.
In the window, from the side of the glass
no one has touched for years
THE SHAPIROS ARE RETIRED
THANK YOU FOR YOUR PATRONAGE
repeats itself,
someone leans to it in the transparent face
looking back at him.
Suddenly his face
touches something, a mouth
or a ghost
establishing itself,
breathing
into his mouth.

18

Last night Shapiro came for me,
hammering out the moist wall
between our houses,
discovered me curled deep in blankets, mumbling
about *men in the red*
thorax of granite, wailing like an unfed baby
as the chisel strokes rang in my ears.

I saw the strong chalky hands of the master
reach through,
I saw, brick by brick, the terrified self
on both sides,
and in a dream where we become
people we have avoided all day long
I heard my name hollowed out finally in stone letters
and my breath shrink away,
a soul whispering to the all, a
wave hissing back into itself against deep salt tons
on the edge of billions of grains.

Strange.
For the first time I saw what was always there—
a sign in white plastic letters hanging
on the door of a vacancy of dust and sharp hammers,
of the half-finished names of strangers.
Strange the way I failed to recognize
myself, amazed, reflected
in a bleak window
behind which others lived, worked hard
and cut out of hard things
what they could,
and polished and blew it clean.

DESNOS READING THE PALMS OF MEN ON THEIR WAY TO THE GAS CHAMBERS

> *Our suffering would be unbearable*
> *if we couldn't think of it as a passing*
> *and sentimental disorder.*—Robert Desnos,
> March 28, 1944, Buchenwald*

Maybe I should go back to the white leather
sofa and bull terrier
of my childhood, when my grandfather died,
but I can't.
It rained and there were beaks of light.
Who was it
picking my hand up where it hung
against my naked thigh?
What matters is how we act before we die,
whether we have a joke ready
and can make all the terrified sad faces
around us laugh and weep,
whether we can make everyone kiss.
Who was it? Who holds us here?
Whom should we touch?

You squeeze my hand.
The orchestra's notes from across the road
weave upward in the smoke,
the frozen eyes, the brown angular light
off center, rows, stacks, glasses
without anyone's eyes behind them
and nothing except
the smile of a boot,
the eyes of gloves,
the mouth of a belt

* It is reported that the French poet, Robert Desnos, broke out of a line of naked prisoners on their way to the gas chambers at Buchenwald and went from prisoner to prisoner reading palms, predicting good fortune and happiness.

and the holes.
Holes.
I squeeze your hand.

You don't love anyone.
I'm sorry. You never loved anyone.
Probably it's because your planets
are mixed, or Jewish.
But there's a cross down by the wrist
on the edge of the mound of Venus
and lines tangling violently
along the third finger.
You're a sexual person.
Still, those lines webbed
under the thumb are bright.
The agony is false.
The earth has been here beneath us
less than an hour
and we are shuffling forward.
Nobody looks at us.
Say anything,
say we are somewhere else,
each violin has
long curved eyes
tilted seaward and up
like your hand in mine.

And yours, little boy with dark brown eyes,
is wetter than the fake soup
of urine and grass the Nazis give us.
You hide your penis fearfully
behind it, making a pathetic cup
while the other hand dangles
like a noose
that will open on no one,

close on no one.
But I predict one last moment of
incredible joy
when you see yourself melt
into the hundreds gasping around you,
and the doors are pulled
and the gas sighs once, reminding
the Father of you.

Nothing is lost. One guard sprouts wings
in his sleep. He is presented a robe of
spun blonde hair and a throne
of tiny nuggets.
In the morning on the parade ground
he opens his fly and prays for us
and is shot
and chopped up for the dogs.
But the next night he returns,
an amputated wing
branding its shadow in miniature
on twelve foreheads.

Like a blind clown I dance between
rifles and the laughter of kings,
and it must be my withered cock and balls,
the color of stone walls,
that cause so much happiness
in the ranks,
as I stumble through the prisoners to hold them,
needing to touch as many as I can
before I go.

There's a shallow hole over the bed
on the wall behind my head
where my dreams live on

after I have waked and knelt
and bled
thousands of times.
I look into it and if I concentrate
I see bodies decorated with
God's toil and ashes.
They drift
into the mouths and eyes
of the living
until there is nothing
but children
like us
here.

Shaggy grains of frost
cling to the ground.
The barracks glitter, the sky hugs
itself like a girl whose arms
have been hacked off, and the wire
hums invisibly in the night air except when a
strand goes white for a second
from no source.
O I want to be that thread, tiny
barrier, bodiless vein, line
that the wind reads.
When I chew on what looks like a finger
and tastes like sour wine
I remember you running, stretching your arms out
to be caught or to fling yourself
through space
until your laughter choked in the sand.
I remember nothing.

You ask me why.
I stand facing you
and speak your name,
whatever it is.

Your name over and over
like a lullaby
until we kiss.
I put my hand on your breast.
It is beautiful, and ugly,
and as empty
as we will be soon.
Lights begin passing
in your eyes
like cities going to sleep
or like those thick lamps on the masts
of fishing boats.
I love you more than I
have loved anyone.
You touch my hair and cry.

Are you different from the one
I just touched? Who are you?
Everyone looks so young suddenly
as if this were the beginning
of the world.
Everything is as silent as this hand
laid up in my palm,
except for a slight hissing somewhere.
What would you say if I spoke?
I will marry a beautiful woman
named Youki,
have children, a cottage
in the forest near Compiègne
and live many years?
I will marry and have children.

Sometimes a message flutters down,
and someone picks it up

and reads:

then goes back home.
The wheels clack.

Unbearable, the wrong parents, the sun
funneling down like the wings
of judgment. Love suffers.
                          I
dance in any direction now,
kissing the guards, soothing their faces
with my torn hands, singing like a child
after a long illness
who is here, here and here,
knowing you by the lost warmth
of your hands
in Philadelphia, Cape May,
New York, wherever I could not be.
Who is it?
I slide under the uniforms
and fill them,
and as I swim the sorrow and depth
of a stranger's blood, of
a belly held in by a bulletproof vest,
I know it was not a mistake
to be here.

I am my sister, but I have none.
My brother, but I have none.

Living men, what have you done?
In a strand
of invisible scorched nerve
scenes we won't remember
never stop flashing toward us,
unreceived,
like us.

The last wisps of gas
rise from our sleeves

and what I danced is danced again where
you smile about love
and eat with friends
the last smile is smiled first
and I am both of them
on the last mouth

and I am the light you see by
fingers tracing the breast
a cloud chilling the street suddenly
what you need, say, lie down
next to in hours
of common terror
I am the face
touch touch

and who it is is who it is

a boot's 0 empties itself eternally
as radiant in the holiness
of presence as
any

I go back
and can't
but I hear myself
call the flesh
call what I love
what I love is not listening

Don't you hear it?
It says "The pain will soon be over"
It says "The lovely season is near"

Don't you hear it?

**THREE**

*. . . Our sages say that there is a death which is
as hard as drawing a rope through the ring of the mast, and
there is a death as easy as drawing a hair out
of milk, and this is called the death in the kiss.
This is the one which was granted to my prayer.*

MORNING

The walls are gone. Sweat burns
in the light.
We are so thin now.
I run my hands over shoulders and legs
and across
necks.
"It was successful"
is whispered into my face
because I spoke to the dead in sleep,
because I lived briefly
like us.
It wakes me. A child's mouth
chews and talks about school.
There is breakfast and the sun entering
colorless glass
and my hands
lifting something, like bread,
like milk that refuses to flow away.
I hear the words meaning
brothers touch like knives
in the first hour.

This soft white country
we have crossed
into so many times
is nameless. Here
wet brutal gods rule,
here dreams
are being cut
out of shoe catalogues and blue swatches
of wool.
Under the same fingers
that touch us, we hide.
The breath of the woman next to me
comes and goes,
her skin cools under the sheets,
her eyes close against
the last room.
But the gold face, the hand-cut
meaningless numbers
grow,
our nights
blow away from us.
There are couples so sensitive
about life they
believe
the hands circling pitifully,
the invisible storm fogging the crystal,
are mouths.
Everywhere
millions of us on each other's throats
ask Who? Why?

SHOES

They arrive each morning
across the blind sex of children,
like the beak of the father who cries,
like the claw of the mother who grieves.
When they curl up
in the wrinkled silence of leather
and begin to move,
it is a sign for us to listen.
Sitting alone at night with my shoes,
I think of the migration
of plucked shoulders, of wings being lost,
and of the nakedness taught
by cattle and stones.
Suddenly wings
fan the windows like ice.
I stare down at feet
and at the webs of torn laces,
long and feathery.

SLEEP

Between tables
and chairs,
between mouths almost
covering each other,
between words steaming
from cells and bones, I
wave goodbye.
I see nothing again but
otherness—chins, cold
negro bushes, mothers in stone,
nakedness without me, wrists
mumbling under the earth.
This light flicked on across the shores
of the body
lasts forever, but not
with money and pain.
This light crossed me
before I spoke,
like the tips of shovels,
eyes wavering through black leaves,
threatening to let in
the whole creature.

Each morning a woman opens the door
and looks
and picks up five bottles of milk.
A faint scraping blurs the air.
Nosebleeds, dizziness, all the signs
of a loneliness nothing can cure,
plague her.
She pours milk for her sons, she
dresses herself and dreams of nothing
in the stuff she pours
and of the great anxiety of
not having enough.
For weeks I have not seen her.
The men drink water.
Who knows what the conversations leave out
or whose mouth churns forever
in silence?

In the neighborhood movies
watching the men of steel and the lovers
and the sacrificial wars
I settle back.
I look for a face.
Pale couples kiss in the long beam of the
auditorium after the lights dim.
Laughter breaks over the faces like rain.
Somewhere hands are moving alone.
And my mother calls, "I told youuu . . ."
My father winks, "She knowsss . . ."
I sit up late, eating a sandwich.
Dust. Images.
The others glide out of me.

GOING UPSTAIRS TO BED

nothing stands in the way
of what the darkness is bringing:
above me, you are a shape
tunneling under a green lawn of wool,
breathing beyond my hands—
the last color bleached out of the tissue
of sense, the last connection
shattered by the last truth, the last grip
on the world spoken by pain,
as it should be, the last houses
in the picture of life on the wall burned
by deaths we wanted and feared and chose
finally, the last resource of love distrusted,
the surf of white cotton
edging out of sight under the blanket
and one hand with an empty web of hair merging
at the top where the hulk babbles and shifts and holds,
and being a man who knows it
and does not know
              someone pulls back the sheets,
gets under and slips into the woman
who sleeps no more deeply than we do
and is kind, always kind, to the naked
lost man who is nothing and there.

step into my room tonight
their hands float ahead of them
their legs move apart
in answer to the many

For thirty-two years I have lived
and known the black iron
railings of houses
instead of you

Now even that part of me
I will never know knows
I have stayed between my own fingers
too long
believing I did not need you there

It is quiet between our bodies
as we open ourselves
to the one shame
and feel what we lose
the wire stems of poppies

Trying so hard to remain
now even hatred is a false petal
shaking under the rain
sacrificed
to the many

For thirty-two years my hands
have wanted to be other things
cups pliers hammers hooks
wings belonging to a child
they touch you.

DREAMING WITH A FRIEND

Your brother is dead.
His breath is one of those lost autumn days
you love.
Your mother works in the kitchen again,
beating eggs.
Ashes drift in from factories,
brush fires
cling to the door.
I see you crossing a field toward me,
not knowing
whom you will find,
kicking weeds.

The dream you told me about is a place
where I touch your head
and you turn.
But I could be anyone.
Your brother sits on the porch again,
crying.
Your mother comes down in the rain.
You see me crossing a field toward you,
not knowing
whom I will find,
following the cracked weeds,
turning as you turn

toward someone.

TO MY FRIENDS

Holding its huge life open to the sky,
snow fringes the scaly cones on this hilltop;
I can see it cupped and pierced by the rich needles.
This far from the city, it takes weeks to melt,
and nothing passes on the road that reaches me here
at the back of my house, planted above the river
of headlights. Do you remember that sad movie
where Bogart loses everything and begins
a new life after his plane takes off through the fog,
where he becomes an underground fighter, and poor?
It haunts me tonight because I am not myself
and, wedged between ceilings and floors,
I can feel the tight path of my hands over the keys
get wider. Because those bare, lasting pines
are understandable, because I am here
and not here, because of the silent breath
rising from different lungs,
because these hands are yours, I remember
something no one will ever tell us. Our life,
more like those trees than we are, is the snow;
the stars know it, the dirt road says it again
each time I stop for a minute and listen to the strange
human words of the hedges scraping together, and go in
where the moonlit weedy spaces continue.

A WIFE TALKS TO HERSELF

A few days ago
my father sent me a box
of wintergreen to replant
so I won't forget him.
I wonder if he saw
the rims of the short notched
leaves get brown
or missed much of the young odor
before he mailed them,
and thought they might look scorched
by the hot passage
from his yard in South Carolina
to this room of mine.
Today, among other things,
I bought soil
and packed it against the roots
of his gift. If that fails,
I'll write him that
there is still nothing more
I can say than this to the message
he gave me through
these wild masks: it is natural
to be shy with one's daughter,
but when I see those curled,
lost faces trying to live
I feel my back stiffen
and remember that once,
passing a stranger
whose thin coat brushed the ground,
I couldn't find
my way home
or recognize myself
in the tiny person
looking at me out of his eyes.

When I pictured you
lifting the old people out of bed,
emptying their pans and glasses,
wheeling them down the hall
and reading to them until their eyes
drifted upward like bubbles,
it was impossible to explain
how you got there.
I began by imagining myself
buying everyone daffodils,
sneaking into the fluorescent ward
after curfew to watch them sleep
and listen as they wheezed
and kept you awake.
And even when I created their dreams
about streets that no longer exist,
and yours about cows and a drowsy father,
that was no answer.
Were you a sentinel
called there to report death
and cancel it somehow,
and if you were God's replacement
what can you say about it?

Late one night, visiting you
with friends, I pushed open the door
where you were staying
and a chalk lady
saw someone who looked back at her
and said Hello.
Tell me, did I speak to a face
or to nature? Who was I trying to reach?
I will go on asking you
what we were doing there
and what you learned
because I am everyone who was not there
and could not feel your thin hands
cup his head into the air
for transparent food
or bunch pillows under his neck,
or see you kneel at the side of a bed
barely dented with the weight
of a human body.
And explain this—each night since then
I have heard the stupidity of the words
you sang out of good books
so they would rest and understand.

ELOISE SIMPSON VISITS THE EAST

Beautiful stupid fat lady, you know everything!
I could see that right away when I lifted your suitcase
and asked was it full of California boulders.
Laughing about your dairy, about plane rides and birth,
you refused dinner. Prophetess of dung and blindness,

I am a religious person too, and drink too much coffee.
Tell me about the city of the gold clouds again,
tell me about your husband breaking horses in his sleep
who can do anything but make money. I dream
as he does about the warm costly trail beneath stables.

In Lancaster, Ollie is waiting for your hands
to fill with her cold tears. It is snowing there.
Through the blanketed windows, you see me trudging
down a street you can't remember. Who asks with his eyes
why you came here? What are you saying to the baby

who acts like a wolf? Thousands of cattle are feeding
on distant grass, tall silver cans fill to the brim
with somebody else's milk. I am talking with your husband
about hooves, ropes, and dust, and as I do you bend to my ear,
red Bohemian millionaire, and say childishly

"His face is so close to the ground!"

UNNAMED SHAPES

Cows have fallen asleep on your land.
Almost late enough
for things from Venus to appear,
night blurs the warm
cellular hulks. Something is between them,
something with fanged eyes
and a hunger. The whispering mounds
grow louder. The grass shortens. You
stay calm among the blunders
of the earth.

For the third time the visitors of love
have crossed our galaxy
to your house
and brought their message.
When they speak to you, you believe.
War stops forever.
Everyone is in everyone, alive.

It would be better if you slept
or continued stacking dishes
by the kitchen window,
and saw your dead uncle's
face steaming out of his grave.

But the light on both coasts is
failing, burning itself out in waves
far from shore and on the shrunken
beaches, like the body of a friend
that is cold. If it is yours,
Ollie, tell those creatures of the
bright planet I am waiting.
Even now I hear "Yes" spreading
out of the shadows of things
around me, long and clear from the
pasture of unnamed shapes.

UNCLE WILL, THE GARDENER

Winter had spoiled his Georgia
because the prize roses in the yard
of the lady who paid him
were dying off. Drunk, guided back there
by a ghost of habitual love,
he dropped his dull head to the first dry
petals he could find, and wept.
Frost netted the stem bottoms
in frail multiplications,
threatening the brittle heads.
Standing at the kitchen door, I watched him,
dressed in the old clothes of three
white relatives, and I thought
there is justice in the economy
of nature, although he can't believe
the death of his closest friends.
A gust ripped the heads off some,
leaving their tall dirty stalks naked,
like markers for the bones of the poor,
and, helpless to change, he began
cutting through the cold talkative flowers,
swinging his arms, bringing down all of them
before the next wind could do it.
Later we spoke of the ice
of this world and of the invisible
destruction that takes what men live for.
I agreed with all he said, but I
heard nothing, understood nothing
except the hilly scar on his cheek.
It seemed, through private sorrow,
to smile and be his true mouth,
not mortal, open to its darkest part,
and coiled something like a rose arched out
just before its petals blacken.

IN THE BLOOD

It is morning on the waters of the self.

I would give anything to kill
the voice that struggles between my ribs
like a ghost being born or like the sun rising,
only to sink deep again into the crust of the earth.
I would give anything if I could leave
the one who eats things with my hands. He's here,
looking for wheat, carrying oil to the North.

I can't help hearing the cries of children.
I still remember a white 2+2.
I still believe it's the answer to everything.
I am not a man and I don't think he is either.

I have looked into his eyes when he was not
looking and I have seen his face plunge through
its country of muscle and nerve and bone
until it was shipwrecked and the wet sand
of his body covered it and he was here,
all here. I am his dog speaking, I fill his eyes,
move closer, tongue of his tongue, teeth, lips.

ABOVE ALL CATTLE

A red clay nude spreads its legs in the early sun.
Her crotch, flooded by the light, has been blunted
and smoothed out. She is forbidden. The poppies
of the Magician droop forward in the circular garden,
and the little house where I must go is flanked
by a sandpile and swings. Whenever I have the courage
to listen, the cries of children float down,
no part of the children. They are gone. There are no games.
The planted walk, the flagstones shadowed with water
from last night's hosing, the seeded new grass
and the trees placed aimlessly, might be called
Paradise, or the place I have dreamt of all my life.
I have come here before, but not like this.
Today the stairs to the upper floor smell like blood,
the window, big as the wall behind him,
blazes like the gold leaf of ages on holy statues
and the branches of the maple, clawing the glass,
are too green, too bright. As usual his face, or the face
of someone I had almost forgotten, blurs,
I blur, something happens to the distance
between us, it shivers, and I think a fist-shaped gland
near my heart has exploded and poisoned me.
Close by, on a baseball field where the grass
has been rubbed level into the dust,
three boys walk toward me,
and a low fence of bushes cutting my face.
Now the roses I knocked over on the teacher's desk
in elementary school flash like the mouths of rifles
a few yards away, where he sits looking out
above the pasture that never fails to produce.
I break like the vase they stood in, I spill out
like the stale fluid that fed their stems,
I bubble up through the skin of a stranger.

It is snowing heavily again.
I have been watching it for a long time
the way a blind man looks at the world
on the back of his eyelids.
Something I wanted in my hands
is not there, and I hear
the soft cry of the flakes approaching.
Trapped among branches,
it sounds as if I have lost someone
and have reached up to find
that same whiteness on my mouth,
plunging into itself without me.

FRAGMENT 122, HERACLITUS

But I was eating dinner with my wife and children
when I heard—You never listen, You never help, You never care,
and saw the old woman with broken teeth sleeping on newspapers
in the bus station and puked when I bent down and touched her,
smelling her mouth, and ran, but You never listen,
You don't know how human we are,
nothing, You never help,
some face mumbling behind me in the night to kill me,
some face burying itself in money and furniture,
I ate another string bean and a hunk of chicken, hopeless,
and the old woman was seen waking and rising like a pale sun
one foggy morning, seen cleansed, singing incomprehensibly
of the life to come when the children we are freely touch us,
but You never care,
house numbers, taxes, what cries out from its pricetag, what prays,
all this wailing hasn't brought You closer, so I go on
watching my children who know much better than You what we need,
my couch is enough of a place to die on,
my bedroom could be one of the green caves of heaven,
even this face,
it listens, it helps, it cares, others have touched it,
but I was eating dinner and when I finished carried my plate
to the sink, went up,
pulled the bedclothes higher on the bodies
of the three girls with nothing on, You dying in my arms,
You in my chest, in my legs, my throat, saying
Sleep well,
forget whatever truths about me break through into the world
but fear this, reading the stories of the day on the old woman's flesh
as she passes over us and smiles down, fear
this "shadow of good things to come."

FOR THE HOLE

It's my parents' forty-first anniversary,
it's the beginning of a poem I was asked to write
by Naptown's wildhaired editor of the perpetual interim
who needs a hole filled in my book.
I wish I could send him a passage from the New Testament
in which Christ doesn't die up there or rise
or say things nobody can understand,
I wish I could tell the story of the dream in the Talmud
where the left eye kisses the right eye, but I can't.
I write page 63, I celebrate at an Italian restaurant
and think of you, like me, stuffed with rolled beef
and greens, eyes, Alcatraz,
God's steel teeth, rugs, suits and tits,
the darkness eating the darkness eating . . .
Thanks for that article about the unborn child
who speaks Arabic and recites holy texts
in his mother's belly—
"The ceremony starts at 5 p.m. when the baby
begins one of his five daily sessions of prayer."
There's a silence in the white faces of snapshots like fear.
I look at one in which a young couple smiles.
Weird anonymous chants of wisdom
from the Surat, like rich food
gurgling in a family's bellies,
are sung.

FATHER INVISIBLE

Don't love anymore, don't be anywhere in the morning,
don't even try to see us from up there cloudy after all we've said,
higher than anything except my knees,
don't watch from the postcards of Nova Scotia,
don't pray like I do for yourself, or was it me
I begged to exist Please Be Here! but don't say Only man is alone,
it's that he feels . . . because if I'm here I die, don't help, don't
heal, my daughters have bad coughs but they don't care,
don't cure them, don't fix the needle on their record player,
they like using the midget rubber lady to weight the arm,
listen it says don't hate hate on the day of atonement,
be some blurred scrawl chalked on the pavement angrily
against the real fathers, old men sitting alone, pale shiny benches,
reading the backward language of God,
who never played with his sons, sleep badly instead, don't
tell us how much love made us steal rubbers from the top drawer
and blow them up, swipe dimes from the pocketbook, it would
kill me if I found out, I'd have big eyes and white clothes
like death, not mercy, not wrath, not the first word
that began everything, we have everything, yellow birds chewing
their cagebars, dogs, "we grieve toward one another" God tells us
"and it could be so beautiful" a little girl, asked about death, says,
if only death could stand noise it would listen to the dogs bark,
it would come back to us and smile and share bread,
people are fighting about who should eat what how much where, O
my glad king of the angels of clarity embrace of what? one
as death unties us like square bundles, One? who
doesn't praise.

AND SO ON

No one has ever named it.
Incomprehensible island
that we recognize and love,
you are strange, like us, like the sun
reaching the top of the sky.

Beyond me, the red grass bends
over tunnels dug for winter;
I am a man sitting down to
a cup of black coffee
and the silence of known things.

Days break open and are, and
everything is understood.
The sunflower seeds I planted
in the shade did not grow, there
is only the elm yellowing

in the distance between me,
the river, and reflected hills.
It's true—I keep listening
to the laughter at the root
of my tongue, and I can't go on.

IN BED WITH MILLIE

I also dream of those I love,
but usually they are suffering along with me.
Anton Chekhov

1

I sleep, I write,
"a light comes from the vegetables."
Rago the fruit man appears in my dreams.
I am biting pears, oranges, tomatoes
and grapes. The juices cover my chin.
What does it mean?
"A light comes from the vegetables
then dies suddenly . . ."
This is one of those nights like
one of those days when I can't touch you
or understand.
I slept early, I forgot to undress,
now I turn and use words and
my hands close on your breasts.
Light, two people, a small man
driving away. I sleep
and wait for morning.

2

You visit me in the hospital
and say "You're the one man
who makes me happy . . ." but
another dream is rage for a close friend
and I hear ". . . mine . . . mine . . ." filling it,
blowing in the air like rain.
Some night when I lie staring over
the edge into the pit of heaven
I'll be rolling toward the flat
overhead lamps and flashing trays,
toward the knot
of green-shirted experts who talk
about little things, alone as the
needle enters me and I
disappear.
Hours later when they wake me
I won't know
which sickness blinded me forever.

3

Now I'm back with you.
My hands rub each other, a
stranger groans behind the curtain
in the other half of the room.
The walls are cold.
Your face drains like the flowers
next to me I can't name,
yellow shaggy-headed amputees.

You sit and stare at the glass pitcher
of ice water
until you recognize a wavy portrait
of me there.
This happens in a dream where those I love suffer.
Your lips open.
Now the dusk has crept in everywhere.
Alone, you smooth my hair
and look out beyond the housetops.
Nothing is there.

4

I know so little about you
but we're naked again
on the roof of a house in Mexico,
turning in the sun until the night frees us.
You stretch out and spread your legs and are happy.
I kiss you like a blind man finding his body.
These days the stone mind of the house is a field
of silence where the roots dream us.
No one has lived there since we left.
The shadows of our flesh
and the faces of leaves and flowers
are the same. Don't you hear this,
nothing but the slow vegetable heart of the land
remembering itself? It says
even night can't erase our ignorance.
The leaves return, cupping their shy flowers.
The veins go to the edges.

AS THE DAYS PASS AND DARKEN

Three nights in a row
I have dreamed about you
living in the house
nextdoor, married, like me.
And each day, after
almost touching your thighs,
I am half asleep.
I began seeing you again
when friends died, or
when a father sickened,
and I wept.
What do I want?
It has been an easy winter,
not much snow,
the same hesitant looks
between people who
would rather touch
and hold each other.
Half asleep, I remember,
and it isn't anything human
about you, it isn't your
face or voice that I need.
I am older. As the days
pass and darken, some-
thing grows too strong in me
and begs on the street,
in rooms, everywhere.

MOTHER POLITICAL

Now I need to forget the pages I can't forget and can't read again
where it says men kill men, men are political forever, life,
our life, a leaflet in the third person, floats into the city streets,
are you listening? On which page does it say You know your life
    enough?
on which page can you find Do this, Not that! Free everyone because
you know enough, on which page is the truth wonderful like your first
    word?
Mother of my mother, clay, sky, this is not a poem, this is not
the ninth page of a book, this is not me or you or a river,
this is not the seventieth bullet that tore through Lorca's right shoulder
before he fell, this is not the silence of those stark telescopic poems
Teresa scratched into her own skin with fingernails that fought walls
and got nowhere with them, with teeth that chewed iron bars,
you can't read them, you can't tell me she said what she said,
because this is how what is never becomes what will be, this is political,
because we're good, we saved everyone, we made mother political,
see her crying when you leave, born for this,
see her laughing in the bathroom to herself when you hit back,

and the bombers are still coming back from Germany, the bombers
still gliding down in Viet Nam, there are still shadows of men vaporised
on walls with their mouths open that the light comes through,
their last words exploded so far back into time
eternity was made longer by them, ferns, memory, clouds, mother so
  political,
you so human,
terrified in bed late at night when the darkness attacked, when
the politicians went down on their knees in the fields of Granada rye
looking for the bullet, wondering how long a kiss should last, hosing
the jailcell so not one trace of blood of shit of a man's puke would be
  left,
and mother so political, us, just us, sitting around, our tiny bird-
mouths open unfed cheeping Not Enough stuffed with pages we can't
  read—
"they were never there, they were not political, they did not sing,
with this volley two dead Spanish angels killed all the starving of the
  world
in their bedrooms because of a girl"—
written so we could sleep political.

ON THE STEPS

I see
a bunch of old Jews sitting around, mumbling
to themselves in prayer,
but I'm outside waiting.
The synagogue's yellow and blue windows tell
the sun's path as I stand there
listening to what must be a hidden song
to the one God.
These past weeks between winter and spring
I have thought of myself walking in, seeking
the blue flame that rose between the hands
of Hasidic masters as they danced, entering it;
being the Rabbi's wife
who hauled two jugs of wine from the basement
for those dry-throated joy-crazed worshippers
whose hands woke God.
I hear
"There's not enough!", her first words
before she saw them, and the silence
I fear somewhere inside me lift its tiny
cry to the name,
because how can I eat love know death die and be someone's other
unless I'm a poor breath chanted into the air through rotted teeth
on the songs of old men?
Well, here I am outside, a man
who can neither share wine nor dance.
Clouds pass, cars pass, people
I haven't seen in twenty-five years speak to me.
Through hard green prongs on a branch, one,
yellow and blown with leukemia, dips his face
to my face.

WILLIAM CARLOS WILLIAMS
READING HIS POEMS

I'm listening to your tired shaky old voice
move in New Jersey over the poems
like ice forming on puddles.
It's sad to hear you sound like that after the strokes,
stumbling, glazed,
after so much raw ball-breaking conversational song.
Spring in Philadelphia, grayish cold, not like
your spring dotted with the blue-eyed flowers
of memory and death, not with a doctor's eye
for the wonder of disease. But there's
snow in April here, like your voice, workers
yelling trustfully at each other, like your voice,
windows trembling in the drone of a huge jet
like your voice nearly cracked by its dedication
to the elements which killed you.
I turn the record off.
In the middle of a poem,
somewhere, either in my mind or yours,
invisible pieces of glass drop to the floor.
I think of Russell's "unbearable pity for the suffering of mankind,"
I think of my sixty-one year old father fantasizing young girls
alone at night in his bedroom.
Hearing you this sunless afternoon
was like walking barefoot across some old starry
floor everyone is afraid of and loving it.

FOR THE GHOST OF LI PO

Tonight in Philadelphia, I saw you, Li Po,
banished immortal,
a poor man who always had plenty of wine.
Tonight I walked down to the Delaware
in the heat of summer
to see if I could kiss your ghost
swimming in rags
among the white leaves of the moon,
that tree without roots
celebrated by the torn fire of stars
on the water.

When Tu Fu saw your eyes flash in a dream
he saw all of us, drunk, liars,
hating examinations and jobs.
Now you drift like the blade
of the new moon behind the masts of tankers,
tall as the shoulders of your children.

I wish Tung-t'ing Lake was nearby
so you could pass it again
on your way back out of exile,

so I could wait there
to ask you for a gulp of the amber wine
of Lu, so we could scale fish together
and roast them
and eat those "tokens of deep feeling."

I can just see you waking up tomorrow
on the porch of your house,
wobbly as a cricket, singing
and brooding until the moon comes by
and breaks in your cup.
I can see you offering a luminous pill
to the Emperor.

Man with nothing after his name,
you think of soldiers smeared on the bushes
and grass of your village,
you thirst for the purple sash,
you drink your guts out quietly,
weeping, failing, watched by four wives,
your hair a long white wave in the Bay
of The Fallen Star.

It's a little thing,
the word my wife says to me
unexpectedly in the middle of a page I'm studying.
But it opens a door
I can't see, don't want to see,
and I turn both eyes in its direction
where a light swells,
where I thought nobody lived anymore.
Remember that spot on the beach in Margate
where there were no people? well,
one morning while you and the kids were asleep
I went there. Thousands of fiddler
crab shells washed up in a border of foam
just above the water, cigarettes too.
I heard the waves hiss as if I had forgotten
how they sounded, and I thought
it's because the sun fell into the ocean.
It was my daughters running down the beach, screaming
"Daddy!", waves collapsing against the jetty,
the word finding its home in the third body
of my mind. Like whose mouth on my mouth
at the beginning of death?
The light has grown over us and covers us
and, I don't know, maybe we'll never understand
"the foot says
because I am not the hand
the ear says
because I am not the eye"

CRUTCHES

Something in me hates being here.
Something in me cuts and sews until the wound
smiles at the knife and the needle.
Something is a wave under the clear thread
and it breaks endlessly.
Something dissolves and opens.
Something always says "No."
How could I have been blind to it for so long?
I can't strangle it or shoot it.
All I can do is talk, when it lets me.
Then silence rots like snow in my belly.
I wait. I look at everything in my room.
I ask childish questions. I call my friends.
Something in me is nothing until I fill it,
but the other mouths of hell wait for this.
These crutches I rub with the sleeve of an old shirt,
this self, these meat-eating flowers,
hate the second me the way God hates evil.
Something is in me forever. Even after
I sleep it goes on using its helpers,
iodine, rain, stitches, eyelids and milk,
whipping flesh until the merciful cures.
What can I do
when it starts again and plunges its claws
into the slush of my lost body and scoops my heart out
and bites it and expects me to rise?
Something never lets me die unless I die.
Meanwhile I squeeze the edges of my chair
and hear "This is happening! This! This! This!"

GOOSEBERRIES

After reading the Chekhov story

I can't sleep tonight, can you?
It is the voice of Gooseberries whispering
we are not good enough to be happy.
Near sleep, when your face gazes at itself
through a window or against a pale floor,
I hear you scratching on the wall of my room.
Forget about happiness. Tomorrow, when we
meet outside on the steps of our houses,
show me how to kiss your sad lips, tell me
what I can give you.
The fat owner who is happy is not you,
eating jam near the glue factory, drinking
tea, bathing in the river,
his wet hands lifted to the dying sun.
In a dish the gooseberries do not wait
and the doctor who did not believe in God
still asks forgiveness, and he is you.
I can smell the clean sheets where Burkin lay down,
suspicious of burnt tobacco.
He thought the stink came from something else.
It was hours before he could sleep and touch you.
Rain beat against the windowpanes all night.

HEARTACHE

After reading the Chekhov story

The horse is breathing on his hands.
The night sky fills his mouth.
It takes many words to say that his son is dead
and many nights to finish,
but the animal is patient. Even the limp flakes
blowing between their heads are a listener,
and riders with troubles of their own,
drunk and in pain and feverish,
are dreaming about a boy they have never met.
Some watch helplessly while he calls and drowns.
Some put a knife into a stranger's neck.
Some twist like keys in a lock on the wrong door.
Some have all the time in the world and a wall of snow.
Some still concentrate on hooves kindling the black street.
Well, the tears of an old man are not important,
especially tonight. Sleep is the one we love.
But a grief in rags leans up to a thick dirty ear
and speaks, and his breath melts a hole in the air
and the years break like infinite mornings on the faces,
white, imperceptibly shrinking, of men asleep
that would not listen.
The rows of stark yellow teeth grinding a slow liquid,
the rasp of a man's throat explaining without words,
the jangle of passengers' coins in a pocket,
something like answers in the jolts of a huge head—
all this continues. Drifts climb under the lamps.

THE KISS

After classes on the Chekhov story

I put my book down and open it
and say ". . . page 53."
Lying on each other like dry skins,
the pages whisper,
my head fills with the sting of
peppermint from a girl's tongue.
The top of the sky turns gray.
We are leaning next to each other
in old steel chairs, we are gray.
Shadows hang in a corner.
The words on the paper, like our breath,
belong to the lost altars of blood,
to a soldier's mouth.
Someone swallows, someone begins to cry.
Ordinary people, ordinary lives.

I have taught this story for days,
my hands leaving the desk to hold something
and offer it as a vision, my fists
motionless on the wood. This anger of
understanding is an empty thing, this
hatred of words because they say something
is a useless bridge between us
when we could kiss.
What have we given or taken, and not touched?
It is growing colder on the windows.
Classes, leaves, clouds, are tearing away.
And now I need strange things to happen—
red moon eating itself in a bottomless mirror,
river foaming under a cabin,
"How stupid! How stupid!" filling a Captain's head.

A LATE NIGHT CONVERSATION

On the hot wall above my desk they flash.
The bare light under them is much too strong
and floods the glossy surfaces. Today
when firestorms bake the plaster where they hang,

eating my brothers' faces, I will look
for those bright figures on the edge of space.
As yet I don't know how, but sinking down
in the fine ash that nothing can escape

my boiled hands may begin to reconstruct
this cheek, that blistered nose, a T-shirt, hair,
and somehow dig until they find the rest.
Right now they hold each other. It is dawn.

Without the light on, the Sierras fade
in one, where Bob scowls, and a green backyard
thins like a winter sky. Phil squats there, drunk,
and Charlie, smoking in his room, looks hard,

and I, well, I just lie back, miles away,
pulling my wire, like all of us, afraid,
because sometimes, in the dark, you and I
break like the silent laughter of the dead.

AFTER TOO MUCH TV

In the glow of the screen with the sound off
I dance, owning nothing, naked,
singing until I become
white mother of the fantasy of love and survival,
God's word!
I kiss my family good night, I
go downstairs to the refrigerator
and sniff earth gasses, farts,
soggy goodbyes, and strip a few bones.
Oh those pleasant deaths in the cold,
unconscious of the last separation
when the tiny hungers suck life back
into the dirt and stars!
I fall into bed.
There is the warm soft cunt whispering to me
almost like a woman, almost like ashes.
On my back
I can go anywhere, I can let go forever
and live in the middle of fire, in silence,
those mad sacrifices the poor make
almost mine.

LETTER FROM A CLOSE FRIEND

This is the last time you'll see me on a weekday afternoon.
I'll be working with the mentally ill in the country.
They have trees there, but not many, and benches,
and I'm told they scream a lot. I want to know
how to help people, I want love, I want their faces and mine
to be the same. So all those hours we spent talking about poems,
complaining, watching each other, I'll be listening to the mad.
I'm scared. Even before I get there I see
the patients rigid and staring under the trees,
the silent ones, some without shoes,
motionless as leaves on a windless day,
and feel myself inside someone I'm afraid of.
A woman repeatedly smooths her hair and I touch her hair.
Her face cracks, she cries "I love you!" for the first time in twenty years.
Long shadows spread into the evening like oil,
and the eyes of those rooted there are veined with light.
It's a strange life out here—fields of sweet grasses, mist,
a word or two, the distances immense between people
as they almost touch, almost speak.
Going in past the fences, I greet them and think of you,
teaching in the city.

SISTER ANN

Come to my room off the street, come into the greasy shadows
of wicker and enamel, into the pierced flaming lips of my mouth,
come out and sit with your hands turned up into my face
over blank linoleum seas, under knickknacks and crosses
and incense curling along paper curtains, come, come
to the impossible infinite eternal perfect great healing
to the powerlady of evil and sickness and bad luck spirits
come to the stink of suffering the fragrance of hope and tin
remover of pain trouble spells death failure ignorance hate
give yourself O man to this lady of the heavenly gift
the trance the lost self the dress bursting with orchids
and the white gypsy blouse the long wobbly breasts the kind
faithful stark eyes of truth come come come to the prayers
of one who has cared is divine come to the Indian of smiles
sit now and listen and see and be given the vision of a self
in the crescent of silence in the black light of the soul
come into the golden smoke the gardenia the velvet the hair oil
where your face drifts like a raincloud or like a wedge of birds
where your hands grow new animal fingers and clutch new things
where you search like dust for a home and are done searching
where the floor swims and the walls come apart and ask you
where the door chants and opens and calls you to fly through
where the window rises like flame like heaven like nothing
now now now now now where she sits like a tumor and listens
where the wise fat of her legs whispers and brings you to
where the daughters of the pig wait where the knives of your bone
where you and you and you and whoever it is have never been
where the bricks begin shifting like words where laughter
where the sty of your cheeks is a desert where stone is the bed
where yesterday shimmers in the rotted fringes between rooms
where the beads clink where the lids pray where the neck shows
where the stockings dance without legs where the toes curl
where the skin falls like a wave where the beach is a good hand
where the sink coughs to itself and leaks into your chest

where the stranger dies with a grin with a straw on his lip
where the naked vein where the talk pours where you change
into where you change where the finger traces the line
where the word and the line are the truth where the nail
where kneelers and askers and failers and hopers and risers
where you find out the miracle of the tongue of red feathers
where everything is you Sister Ann where the crotch is burning
where the green secret numbers flash on the wall and mix
where all my friends have gone have been healed and are saints
where my mother and father have gone not to die and are living
where my children are sent and are better and are glad, still,
where the teachers die and the masters die and the dead die
where the pencil spills its lead like a blizzard over the city
where the bottle of milk turns to an ocean of permanent ink
where the how and why are a furnace of bread and metal
where the poor shine out like gold coins and the rich are weeds
where the tree sings and is fed where the hills are merciful
where the morning creeps like a turtle into my endless laughter
where the crow and the dove breed for the future of men
where no one weeps where no one laughs where no one speaks
where the earth spins like a corpse in the old speckled abyss
where I remember everything the tennis court the arrowheads
the trips the smell of dresses the grades the cheating the sperm
the bicycle the crib the rainy day when he died the bad heart
the vomit the checkers the ass of a naked parent the stolen toys
the beatings the friend burning the insects the light the soap
the new shoes speaking the oracular yes
where anger anger is the name of everyone you love where the carrot
and the potato are sprouting on the windowsill
where you are tiny where the dog and the ant and the goldfish
are closest where the sheets turn like ghosts against your desire
where the closet is a box where the toilet is infinite
where the child tumbles forward and has nothing to hold
where it is never tomorrow where the mirror is empty forgotten
where plans are a lie where people are you where you are
where you are always lost where she begins again her predictions
where she does what others call impossible all the way back into

No one is here today, the streets
fill with rain, drops echo in long puddles
near the walls. I am talking to you again
but you don't hear.

In my childhood there's a room
where I sit in bed listening to the radio, un-
raveling the edge of a blanket with my lips. The blue
twilight ceiling, heavy and soft as wool, trains
jumbled in a box, a tin
horse galloping forever,
then sleep—I think about this often.

Like now
without anyone. Tell me what your life is like, call.
Sometimes I dial your number in a rich Jersey town
and can't speak. I know what to say,

but there are
times when I'm sure I can
cross the street and go up and find you
sprawled on the floor studying, playing records,
smiling because I'm there. There are times,
and we grow distant over the years, and live
somebody's life, ask nothing, and live.

Thirteen faces waiting to be born
and nothing to say on this Monday morning,
the schools closed, rain, the new killing.
What do the crickets hear when I lie down on them
in the grass? My hands sinking?
I'd go to Jesus Christ like Arina, the woman
from the Hotel Madrid in Babel's story who was knocked-up
and beaten across the belly with a belt
by Seryoga, the janitor, I'd talk to God
like she did and hear Him say "You cannot kiss
your own ear . . ." and be turned into an angel
with wings made from the sighs of babies,
I'd fuck the father of my child until he smothered
and Christ cursed me for killing one of His angels,
I'd make Christ weep for me, like she did,
if I could bring us back,
because who else does this kind of thing?
who else needs to be forgiven?
This morning we decided to list our bad dreams
in a letter to Nixon, beginning "Dear Mother,
we don't like these dreams, we can't stand them,
we know you caused them, we want you to take them back . . .
signed thirteen students without wings
who have arms that don't lift,
feet that lie flat on the ground and freeze,
hands that tremble and go nowhere,
lips as tender as the passages of birth,
anger in the snapping of wings."
I'd put my mouth against theirs but they don't breathe,
and it goes on like this,
I'd lift up each skirt and let my head slide back in,
like disciples who worship revelation in The Mother,
asking "Is this the wound, is this . . .?"

87

JUSTICE

. . . which is the mystery of mysteries

The children are upstairs, but not sleeping.
The young one cries
". . . my doll's neck!" and the other screams back.
The air is so clear I can see the veins of leaves
which don't move, neighbors gliding in their rooms
through the blue auras of TV bathing everything.
Words float out, clear as the heavens tonight
and as mysterious.

Through these windows, through the bones of the person
I sleep with for years, through the first
veil wrinkled over the glued sight of the fetus,
irises adjusting to the light on things
that pours in and keeps back nothingness,
what do I know?

I want to lie down next to you
and know and be known, and say nothing,
face to face with my own clumsiness,
and bite on the sweet patch of hair between your legs
as it darkens between us when we touch.

There are pictures of me.
In one I lean on my hands and look for you, just angry
enough to make you feel you didn't give me something
I needed very much.
In another I'm outside against a red wall
torn by sunlight and leaves.
I grin, my crazy exploding hungers lash out to escape death,
I'm chewing a hand that hides the flesh
of the real God that can save us.
In the last I just lie back on a sofa
and don't give a fuck what you do or what you say or what
anything is. Wars deepen and grow quieter

because who knows, because
not one breath moistens the air tonight
or clouds the stars, because the moon is,
because this mouth wants to put food into your mouth
and fill it, because is, is, and is,

and won't stop laughing.
                    The dark weighs.
What is the tongue for when the voice is gone?
The sky glows like the faces of children.

WHAT HAPPENS

By morning a thin black dust has covered everything.
Evening and more bad news.
I feel closer to my friends than ever,
and more afraid.

Gray puffs under the eyes,
sprays of darkness at the corners of the mouth,
a silence wasting its last hours on me,
and I don't understand.

Messages from the insane jailed prophet of Cleveland
wake me, screams of the punished come down,
my sleep fills with stabbings and helplessness,
and I go to work.

Yesterday I walked through a supermarket with a friend,
but I was reading in bed, I was alone.
I turned page after page in a small book,
like wind shaking the windows, and I wept.

But I know the full skies of onions protect us,
the mushroom is rubbery and strong, tomatoes
signal from a long way off, and each grows
peacefully, ripening until it dies.

This has no meaning, this doesn't explain
the growth of dreams, teeth grinding the air,
mouths hypnotized to say these things, or
what happens.

NICK'S PHOTOGRAPH
OF JEFF, ME, AND ARLENE

The grass is white, a void we could slip into
if we stepped back. The leaves are gray fires.
The open picnic basket, cartons of milk,
people standing wordlessly in a field—
nothing explains why it is like this.
You wear a stained hunting jacket from a time
when you went crazy and needed a hobby.
You look angry because you fear being alone.
You worry about how not to be eaten
by the suspicions of love. In this outing
everyone is facing the camera, a thermos
leans into the light's edge, and no one knows
what drew us here on a wet summer day.

CHARLIE'S PHOTOGRAPH OF MILLIE

I keep staring at your bent figure in a field,
all the grass burning, everything the sky.
But you curl forward and smile and don't mind
what I feel will destroy you. That's how you are.
The pit of shadow above your head
could be the gate of life, or the chill
of a lost wing, or a memory that won't leave.
Sunlight eats your hair, your mouth
whiter than this page when it was blank,
the back of your head blinding me so
it's my face, and I sit here wondering
what it is about love that does this.
You seem to be going. You seem not to care.
This landscape tacked up over my desk
as if it knew me—I can't say what it knows.
I can't stop looking at it. I keep it here.

WANTING TO BE HEAVIER

People are chewing on wood.
All those letters about ourselves we mailed to friends
have been collected and sent back and huddle
on doorsteps. All the words have died out.
The blind silent anger that lifted pens
and dragged them across paper is all that's left.
This is what happens when the parents wake up.
This is the revolt of the ghost fathers
who got less love than they needed from their sons.
This is how wives live forever after the marriage battles.

Now there's nothing for me but the last saint's hair, flaring
like a star, nothing except distance and prayer.
Now those who listened are trying to write back.
They drift into my eyes as the sweet clouds from bakeries,
they choke me with the sour breath of cars,
they have signs plastered on walls that the rain licks.
Wanting to be heavier, I do bad things.
I build statues of my mother with putty and salt.
I talk only if the wind rattles a flag or sings through a keyhole.
I gnaw pencils and print my name.

SECOND BIRTH

Women are watching their dogs fight.
They're so close they could be wounded by the curved nails
and fur, by the clouds of anger, by the teeth,
but they just stand there chatting, looking up,
dusting their shoes. I often think of the wives I know,
alone during the late morning hours of the day
with nobody they love, glancing lazily
into a hall mirror, seeing nothing there but the room.
What can they do? They look off into the air, they clean.

No children crowd the schoolyard, they read.
One leg puddled with gray milk, one bloody,
one matted with the grim silence of oil—
in classes even the boys are taught, like wives,
that it's better to choose pairs and hit and divide
and make food small and not ask or cry for love.
Rain glazes the iron fenceposts endlessly.
The cinders bloom. Second birth, it's all the second birth!
What promise can stop this, whose pain will try?

ON THE HANDLE OF THE WHIP

Cold coffee. I was sitting around thinking about my brother,
I was dozing near the TV, drinking cold coffee,
listening to the street, thinking about my thoughts, seeing
Jesus, mother and father and the secret poor, seeing blown
kid's guts in America, swarms of helicopters fluttering down,
God's car bodies, Apollo's pure light, bone,
all the revelations of this age. And I heard John's great
"I am the door. By me, if any man enter in, he shall be saved."
And I saw my enlightenment in the scowl on Agnew's face.

Last night I dreamt Philip Levine was a tall Chinaman.
In a room with windows on the ceiling and no chairs
we sat and drank cold coffee and wore hats and he showed me
the nineteen Chinese Position Books in which Heaven & Hell
are drawn with colored silk thread, just like my father's.
"Don't let this country fuck your head," he wrote from Fresno,
"I had a nervous week, down, the old stomach trouble."
And I knew this poem was about the disasters of standing up,
about the miracle of having scaly six-eyed relatives.

THE EXTERMINATOR ON SCHOOL

Friday, he knocks "Can I come in and spray, Hello!
can I give it to the bugs, don't worry, move." He's in.
"OK but don't spray my feet, I'm a bug but
I want to live, I like this . . ." He is the white-faced old
anxious nut babbling "I just sprayed a high school, God,
you should have seen those dirty monkeys climbing around
everywhere, it's accredited too, scared the shit out of me,
it's accredited, I can't believe this country, how
can they let a place like that with those hairy creeps . . ."

No sun and the last day of the work week, Bill
sitting down with a drink weeping again, marriage, hope,
this nation of exterminators running for President
of nothing, us carrying tanks of poison
on our backs with a rubber hose and a long nozzle, dying
to kill those armored creatures that nuzzle our toes.
We want to be floors, we want much more, no more, fire, bottles,
we touch hands like little girls in a circle screaming "Don't! Don't!
don't let that sticky gook get on me!"

AWAY FROM THE OCEAN

Sunday in Philadelphia, without love.
The TV goes, one killing after another,
in another room. I see women
sitting alone like me, talking to themselves,
and men clipping their nails in strange rooms.
Nothing is more dangerous than being human.
An open loaf of bread turns stale in the kitchen.
I have said nothing all day, hated money's power
and thought the war was ended, and lived.
Last week I stared at the Atlantic for hours
and at a few hungry gulls diving for food.
I was afraid. The waves flowed in.
The sky changed invisibly. It grew cold.
I could hear someone crying above me.
And I remembered that very old poem about gods
who eat men, whole mountain ranges, anything
they need. The beach was red. I shook.
I drove back to a strange room.

THE RETURN OF BLACK SHAG

It was a cool night in Philadelphia
when I saw her, drunk, with a bag of peanuts
and a baby, under the streetlamp.
I thought about walking up and saying "Let's"
but then I saw her cape with the green felt letters
spelling out BLACK SHAG,
and I froze. "Black Shag," I said to myself,
the world's wildest lay club.
You had to be a strong guy to just walk up
to a member of that club. I waited.
I felt around for one of my blue pills.
I lit a cigarette, coughed, but she was still there.
I decided to do it.
A few steps and I was next to her, smelling
her breath of chocolate and come and grave dirt,
staring down into her transparent dress
at the huge boobies. Slowly I let one hand
slip into her blouse, slowly
I lifted her skirt, and she just stood there
with the peanuts and the baby.
Before I knew it I was in, hammering
like Batman, Robin, Captain Marvel and Superman
all doing it to Wonder Woman.
Suddenly I knew I would never be the same.
This was the best, this was one of the big ones.
I would never forget Black Shag, America's
greatest Queen of The Quick Lay, holding tightly
her peanuts and baby, with a tear in her eye,
shouting—"It's Love! It's Love!"

The most fantastic poem in the world
can't save us. We'll be teaching and suddenly—
bombed in the chest; we'll be screwing
and suddenly—both balls drop off, or we'll
find the left half of our brain shut off
and the right trying to keep us going like a cane.
The most fantastic poem in the world
is our death, and it won't help to cry,
it won't help to sit down as if someone
hit you in the mouth with a dog.
The most fantastic poem in the world
is a bag of horseshit, like this, or like
cotton candy on the tip of your nose,
or like Charlie finding out he has
a disease called "the inner kiss is a warning,"
like Jeff, diagnosed as fatal, with
"a cloud of mice has announced cheese runs,"
like Bill who found out with his own knife about
"the motherbird weeping and drowning us,"
like Desi who, it was obvious all along, has
"the endlessly stiffening leg in the bushes,"
like Nick, wooden-handed Nick, who we know now has
"white rising wings of the liquid insight,"
like Reds who saw in a dream his future as
"the smile crippling and squeezing it past,"
like this horrible incurable thing called
"fingers keep swelling like watermelons
in Alaska, in Philly, in the middle
of the most fantastic poem in the world."

Maybe I should be happier, at least
I'm not Kafka frozen to his bed by a huge wax lady
who won't leave,
but I wake up thinking about the President
I don't have, about Alaskan oil I don't have,
about the castle with its own crocodiles and chains
I don't have.
All this nonexistence haunting me not Kafka
and sex merely the last form God takes before He dies forever.
Maybe what I mean by "happier"
is evil not Kafka,
a Jewboy without underpants or guilt.
Maybe this bread maybe that road,
maybe rain maybe the sun.
How much faith must have died when I emerged,
how much blindness when I first looked,
and it continues like the two white fists of a father
who asks "Which hand?"
and I open the left and there's nothing
and I open the right and there's nothing.
Smiling becomes my passion not Kafka.
I sleep in traffic in the middle of conferences,
the lessons I give become clouds not Kafka,
lunch is the knowledge of Kafka not Kafka.
Unfortunately
happiness is easy.
For many nights this keeps me awake
and the revelation of forgiveness lets its beams crawl over my face.
Now I think,
when a neighbor shows up in the night and tells me not Kafka,
no maybe
I'm not close to your pain,
your weak remedies, maybe not,
maybe it was nothing like this, no light, no tears not Kafka.

A GLIMPSE OF THE BODY SHOP

They are inspecting hearts again.
One slips a fat needle into the left side
to judge the color,
another weighs it, one with goggles on bends
over the scars and black coins
and cuts off ragged strands for the analyzer.
For years they have known about the region
called Moon Breakage,
but grow silent when asked.
Nevertheless it haunts them.
And today, with the tables dripping
and because so many brought theirs in
to be checked,
one of them presses his to his cheek,
one begins chewing the large artery,
one kneels and holds his up to the sky,
one jams his fingers into each hole.
But among all these I stand
aside, doodling with chalk, trying
to bring together the sad details.
Suddenly a wall of the garage
is filled with the weird cry of chalk,
many letters and signs appear.
The one man capable of this sits down,
exhausted and proud.
His helpers wash and bow, laughing.

DIRECTIONS FOR BEING JESUS

If I used everything but the names
it would mean photograph me carefully
taking my belt off at the opera,
tell the story about my boils and loans,
add me suddenly to the war budget,
put my hand over your mouth like a strong wind,
study my eyes instead of Chinese Art,
listen to my hair instead of the radio,
make your "against" against "for" and your worst
dream about Bibles and armed boys my dream,
elect me to the Presidency of Small Teeth,
cause me great accidental pain in the kitchen,
strike against what it costs to support
my wardrobe and my imaginary diseases,
put cremation on the list of possibilities,
say how easy resurrection is, how Jewish,
read me on the toilet, on airplanes, in bed,
lose me on a trip to the parental estate,
drop me at timed intervals in the caves,
call me a human footnote to the enemy's essay,
write down SB on your list, not radishes,
be disappointed in the size of my breasts,
say my robes are ugly, my skin, they cover
a heart in a feminine chest that coughs,
lift my head from its pillow and kiss it,
say how bad these old photographs of us are,
how Christian the invention of film is.

FOUR

DARK LORDS WHO WAIT UNTIL THE CHILDREN EXHAUST THEMSELVES

houses have roots like trees, people have
roots like warm stones, cities
have roots like stars blazing in six directions,
nations have greed at the root, and the
huts tremble

I came out from eternity, my mouth struck
by an angel's hand, fable of the mother of God who
looked into her child's mouth, saw the universe
was blinded and forgot
                              this face of mine
not by itself alone but in my brother's face, lives
to eternity
in mud and fire

now when the rescue siren pierces the night
I wish I could go back again
                              and
ask what it is to be home, what it is to
sing forever through the lighted dusts, to be a lost mouth asleep
in the rubble of the sky
                              the scaly newt
creeps from the stone & the armed fly springs from the rocky crevice
the spider the bat burst from the hardened slime crying
to one another   What are we

                    •

in the market place at the center of the city
anything was done, all buildings and all actions
no secrets between the citizens and friends, no walls

the mind dawning on chaos
                              comic slang tragic dignified howl
river valleys where the city first multiplied
not buildings but men until the regression to utopia

for the city of the dead came first, caves, mounds, living in the body

like Mexico today relatives sitting around the graves
sowing marigold petals everywhere
making crosses out of the petals
getting drunk on top of the dead

                ●

56 Conestoga Indians buried in Washington Square mixed
with the other dead under the
shadow of the Hopkinson House
those who hid in a Lancaster jail were killed
many who came to Philadelphia for shelter
died of smallpox
those who escaped ate wild potatoes near Wyalusing Creek
                                                              but

when the snow melts
so long behind walls we can't remember
what it is to be at ease
when I think of squeezing into the world
and slipping out
on the same bed
and of the lost roads of water inside everything
what can I do
let me into you for awhile
brown vacant trees
cripple singing to itself in a cold room
warm us

•

Aristotelian misery Plato's dream of a house without windows fresh air
artificially purified pumped by machine

I have spoken to the walls to the air friends mother and father to my wife
and told them who I am

how can the city exist without it
men working at small tasks cooking
sweeping washing their socks buying flowers
dressing their children reading to them at night
spackling a wall stories about the monster and the prince who feared
    death and darkness
who hated being alone and
hacked with both arms into the scaly heads
still alive invisible snorting fire

all the stories in bed and the stories my daughters tell me
about the world inside them and outside
mean so much, about how much lemonade they sold on the front steps
    yesterday
clam shells a doll's eye rolling under the bed artificial stars pasted
on the ceiling

•

1682, "having a light and dry bank next to the water
with a shore ornamented with a fine view
of pine trees growing upon it ..."

O it's bitter to be human and use words

where the moon pulls the small tides of the belly
the huge tides of the earth
the coiled torn gigantic star beaches
into a single breath

the dirty hands of children eat what they hold

●

Nineteen days of pure anger without God
full moon wafer of silence
hatred things asleep cold
grass leaning on itself
howls
I can hear the old mothers of the wind at sunset crying
strangers waiting to step inside
and wash
and curse themselves in the mirror "in 1747, John Harding, a miller,

built a wharf and made a windmill on the muddy island
against the town. However, he took a fever by working in the mud, and died. The windmill operated for a
few years when a violent gust blew off its top and sails, carrying
them to Joshua Cooper's orchard on the Jersey shore. There it
was seen as a place where boys played for many years after."

"in the place where the mill stood, a bakery and a tavern
that sold milk were built" we made love we slept

moon in the river
in the hidden cells of the leaf in the eye

●

The police chief's wife longs to be lifted into the stars
who will volunteer, cup his hands on her ass
as she stands on a wobbly ladder in the kitchen fixing curtains
she sleeps badly wakes to look at the man beside her
nail the rods to the windowframe hold her up
the sun blasts into the sink insults
the young shout at cops

•

Oysters love glass
many are dragged up sucking on a bottle
those are the fattest ones
but if you shift them from one bed to another
make sure the second is fresher
or they will die
when the dredging machines work they
drag oysters to a new bed
increasing their field
"It is a false kindness to let them alone, to
protect them . . ."
mud destroys them
disturbance multiplies them

•

But who? your mother who calls up
to tell you about her childhood

                    "You know I've had a lot of death. My
                        whole childhood was
full of it. When I was three a girlfriend of mine was
run over by a burning oiltruck. She died. Another
friend died of a brain tumor. My brother, a Christian
Scientist, died of TB when he was 26. He could
have had a great career as a concert pianist. Rheumatic heart. My
mother had headaches which forced her into bed. She'd
walk around the house with her head wrapped up in a black rag."

Mother, I don't mind listening to the angel of death but
three days later part of me kills part of me

"Your own self lives in the hearts of all. Nothing else matters."

This is what you get at the feet of one of those Hindu assholes—
wisdom—

109

useless as a broken shoelace, from the Forest Debates.
I haven't seen a real forest in 20 years.

Or
"In this body, in this town of Spirit, there is a little house . . .
and in that house there is a little space. One should know what is there."

The feet of the Master Aitareya stink and peel
the feet of the Master have long horny toenails
the feet of the master are crooked and dry
the feet of the master don't move anywhere
the feet of the Master have crummy old rags on them
the feet of the master don't even wiggle
the feet of the master could easily be mistaken for wood
the feet of the master have cowshit spattered on them
the feet of the master are like the hands of someone idiotic
who has worked all his life to built a heaven out of dust, snow

Ugly!!

     ●

Afraid standing over the fishtank dense with
carp, their fat gray bodies twisting, their mouths
pursed eating shit

"You want to be a fishman, learn the names of the fish?"

But the man chops off their heads
scissors the fins
sweeps the scales off with a scraper

in a tunnel between the nunnery and the monastery in San Angel
archaeologists from Philadelphia found

over a hundred mummified infants smiling out of the clay walls
staring eternally into God's merciful face

one fish tries to jump the tank
as I buy one have his bones flipped away
the clay smiles
                    only the angel of death knows the answer
and he is hiding behind God

"The Vietcong take the toads, tie their mouths with string
and throw them into our camp. When they croak, our soldiers
mistake the croaking for men's voice and we open fire."

And to the angel of the Church in Philadelphia write
he that openeth and no man shutteth
and shutteth and no man openeth
                    from *The Book Of Masters:*
"If I were married to you, around
May 15th I'd sneak up on you with a huge mallet
and hit you over the head and then revive you in the middle
of September. In the meantime I'd have the airconditioners
going full blast all summer and you would have been
sent off with the rugs."—Reb Parker over the telephone

                    •

Laughter is the trunk of love magic,
Aceldama, the field of blood, is where the evil ones' bowels gush out.
Is it the same as God's "I will pour out my Spirit upon all flesh."?
Is it the same as whose cock is bigger, who can do it the longest?
Is it the same as did you eat her, did she go crazy?
The same as thumbsucking before the void takes me,
and the wishes—to eat to be eaten and to sleep—are
teeth to bore back into the mother.

Is it the same as Bwebweso! He is a tame prick! He has never killed a
   man!?
Sleep with the pressure of shit and water on your head.
Sleep like a log your dick like her nipple in the sky.
Like the Beautiful Wing Meadow, like the Story Of The Light That Dis-
   appeared.
Like the shark that was gutted and used as a canoe.
Like jerking off without guilt, the end of the world originally.
The same as the city formed out of the dreamer's body,
the reason for dreams, not to lose the body, the new city?
Use this as a curse, like your mind, use this
as sauce as meat as the dumb triple figure inside your head,
use this as a chant for falling asleep quickly,
at least.
The great Father Snake smells your foreskin. He is calling for it.
You better use this!

   •

Governor Dennie's daughter was buried in the Friend's burying ground
near the corner of Third & Arch Streets
after she had been dead 30 years
she was dug up and found all in one piece
but fell apart when she hit the air
her hair had grown as long as the grave-digger could extend his hands
what nails!
and her dress was in such good shape the grave-digger's daughter wore
   it
silk!
it outlasts lead coffins

and all over Philadelphia
10   15   20   25 feet underground trees leaves nuts
were found standing on end pines laid out
hickory spatterdock oak oysters slime from the sea

fish living in branches people's eyes bones hair
stuck on things wild Virginia flax gravel bottles
filled with wine beer that was still strong

heaven & hell paradise the old populations we miss so much
grieve for imagine even speak to in our brains
are living a fairly good life next to the *rock of steel* five tons
that fell through the bottom of a collapsed furnace
"and all are quite unconscious of the treasure that rests beneath them"

drowned men warriors bugs amethysts topaz kids buttons tiny veins of
    gold
the depths Poe knew in
                    "a scorn of all things present"

      •

"O final mission of the city
to further man's conscious participation
in the cosmic & the historic process . . .
through emotional communion
through dramatic representation   to put the gods in their shrines"

in the river valleys

"I don't want to die, I want to watch cartoons." my daughter, one
of the few honest people left, tells me at breakfast

but the Texas billionaire O giant American tit money does not contradict
God money does not need anyone except more money
inky tit of the poor sweet gland of the industrialist banker investor
sinking his cock into the oil field

1500 young Americans wait in bamboo cages
Bethlehem Steel paid no taxes last year this year I owe the govt. $544.34

Cartoons? French fries you can trust?

> "Men die nightly in their beds, wringing the hands of ghostly
> confessors, and looking them piteously in the eyes—die with
> despair of heart and convulsion of throat, on account of the
> hideousness of mysteries which will not *suffer themselves* to be re-
> vealed."

see a god on every wind & a blessing on every blast
or hear sounds of love in the thunderstorm that destroys our enemies'
    house

No good at all: but my grief is stronger than I.
Love of the dead is bitter, I know, and strong.
. . . I am nothing . . .
No man can deny you have lost a devoted wife.
And there is no more pleasure for me in anything.
Time will take care of that.
Yes, if Time is Death.

Well, I've given up being a Rabbi because I think they're going to arrest
    us someday
for making weird poems for fucking too much or too little for leaking a
    few drops
in our pants given up being a Rabbi because they're like Jewish Presi-
    dents, or
steel company Presidents without hands—unheard of!

CHILDREN

When the children see each other eating ice cream
they all smile and they all seem happy
when the children touch each other's tongues together
they giggle and laugh and play around
when the children run out of classes at the end of the day
they fill their hearts with joy
when the children go home into their houses

they take their clothes off and go swimming
when the children watch television
they all go up in the air because there's no gravity because
the TV makes them scared and all the gravity goes away
when the children eat dinner with their father and mother
worms are in their meat jellyfish in their milk
crabs in their beans giant people are stepping on their feet
when the children sit outside on the steps in the twilight
they play kickball with their father the sky is moving away
they eat peanut butter
when the children take a bath
they splash and dance in the tub and think about diving
when the children crawl into bed
they think about ghosts and eagles and demons in the forest
in their dreams and scream all over the house and go crazy
when the children sleep
they wiggle snore push their covers off the bed they wake up
dizzy
when the children eat breakfast the same thing happens
and even our death is forbidden

and I see that thumb enter Nixon's mouth when he's alone plotting our
    future
I see him creating the history of man with his dog there licking his feet
    O Master
I see his perfect daughters putting flowers in vases feeling ecstatic
    about power
unapproachable right smiling on all
his wife powerless to know you
I see advisors refusing to cry on their wives' breasts the tears falling
    backward inside until they reach the intestines like the mouths of
    acid eat through
holes breaking into the inner skies of blood

I see Agnew shaking his head after a hundred missed shots on the
   tennis court who hates to lose who can't understand how he could
   miss
and wants to eat his opponent

I wish they would give up and become insurance men perfume salesmen
   or open flower shops
like the Mafia
death is forbidden so they cause death, the spectators are maimed
as in C. K. Williams' great ugly poem after the Kent State murders
his horrified child's voice screaming against his own broken head
my refusal to hear it

some small tobacco shop or fruit stand where they can cheat people
   harmlessly

                    ●

the city is moving like the womb, slowly, without knowledge
                                                   because
the body is with the King, but the king is
not with the body.
                 because
no people sing with such pure voices as those who live in deepest hell;
what we take for the song of angels is their song

of
   before falling asleep felt on my body the weight of the fists on my
      light arms
of
   10 bloodcells per microscopic square
of
   Ockene a cross drawn with magic markers on his belly where he was
   pinpointed for radiation spleen bulging liver bursting
   eating fruit blood beginning to weep in anger through the skin
of
   a bag of fruit on the windowsill in his room
   is he dreaming about roots?
   does he have food?

of
  Black Elk's pure "So many other men have lived and shall live that
      story,
to be grass upon the hills . . . for these are children of one Mother and
      their Father
is one spirit."

The abortionist from Canada leans on the fender wants his money now
behind the Chinese screen he inserts a pellet
hours later she is bleeding to death
for 200 dollars

                    •

story of a mighty vision given to a man too weak to use it
and of a people's dream that died in bloody snow
and this hide upon the mouthpiece here from whence we came and at
whose breast we suck as babies all our lives

the end of the dream is a vision of the other world which is here
sun that does nothing but give
table you eat on chair that holds you up laugh
it is The Face forget everything put
this together
all the leaves as you sat by the water knew the miracle and forgot

                    •

Children love God. They don't know Him.
They talk about Him, they are His friends.
They ask.
Any answer is right. They love the angels. They play
and see dogs riding bicycles, cats with wings,
black ships searching through the night with a long ray.

found myself crawling up a hill talking not hearing myself

dreamt of running away with her
all her money in my bag
                    the worst results flow from parents who have kept them-
selves artificially unconscious

More. More. Nothing, so much nothing. Refrigerator light. Squeezes his
    face
and wonders is it mine? Do I need? Is yours yours? Didn't write my
    name on
the Easter hat like my kids . . . love for which it is hard to find a name
in the language of man.

RO 8–7902
AH 2–3008
RM 4–7783
ML 9–5939
RN 2–2554

Call one of these numbers & ask any question. The answer you get will
    be the right one.

                •

What do children lose? Teeth? Fear of being alone? The skies they
fall from, silence, the first spirit of God?

billion of lights in the birthwaters
swim with the white veils of creation over their face
their transparent hands open on the great cord
of all to all

•

if only he could lift himself from this bed, and I am lifted and kissed
if only he could understand death, and it understands
if only he could go home, and I say going home

and the waters calm the sky clears the face of the man in bed
calms in a strange building suddenly breathes out and flattens and is
    eased backwards
between

the grief of those who are standing
insult of silence from the man who will sleep forever
talking trying to raise him with speech
yourself

wound we believe and
the silence of the God whose spell of silence cast into the body of the
    one you love
is it nothing?

•

My youngest daughter hands me a drawing she did in school this morn-
    ing
a girl beneath orange clouds
smiling
on a green field edge to edge
with a huge eight-pointed sun lighting it up
blue mouth blue eyes
and on top a dark blue sky edge to edge

lunchtime suddenly a monkey appears on the fire escape
jumps at the screen lost
wonder in the middle of the city
his dull scabby ass thrust out at us
he wants to enter the family again angry little man
us
tinyheaded
lost
he holds on to anything he can't fall
"Everything improves," Chekhov said.
the kids screaming Gorilla! Monkey Church! Monkeys riding on trains!
   Wearing shoes!
Dining!

my wife says he looks Jewish

                    •

Am I the one I want you to want me to be?
Am I the one I think you want me to be?
Am I the one you don't want me to be?
Am I the one who wants himself to be different?
Am I the one you used to know?
Am I the new one who is the one he is?
Am I the one you think you are?
Am I the one you imagine I think you are?
Am I the one I want you to think I am?

can eat in the library during weekends if they put down a cloth
watch for Betsy's phonecall
snow plow man comes automatically

extra door keys in duck on patio
Betsy has own key
leave Bets bathroom light on at night
milkman also has eggs juice butter if you get stuck
kids take turns doing dinner dishes
use both fans when you cook

•

what friends do in my sleep is
a baby raising a baby
mother making a father
father making me a mother
pigs grain jewels silk corn splashed at their feet
they threaten themselves with the KingQueen images
they wear skirts call themselves Daddy

•

Every morning CK calls before 10
"Miss Torpey hated me" he says
with her torpedo-shaped breasts

from *The Book Of Masters:*

> "The shoes, like, they should have feet in
>   them,
they're empty, the light comes up out of them, it's scary with no one in
    them.
That's ridiculous!"

It passes, it passes
>   the breaking pain in the thighbone passes
>   the ulceration of the skin passes
>   the big black evil of the abdomen passes
>   it passes, it passes

and the war surrounds us like the fluid we drank grew up on inside her
we'd fuck ourselves to death in the Greyhound Bus Terminal without war
we'd invent pockets with slits for our hands to go through while buying
    steak
we'd splash like grapefruits against a wall from too much love
we can't live without the black fires of war lighting our emptiness

Miss Torpey, I should have known you were the God I needed
how could I have become the great cripple I am without you?
how could I have lived? How could I have wanted to kill love?

Churinga—one's own hidden body, the double of himself, a stone penis

•

Under the waving trees, flowers blow, the voices
of a man and woman, tall white cumulus riding across,
something on the radio from another time
>   I see veins on top of my hands
bulging ageing an ache in my shoulders & my left eye
the Gemini 8 photograph of the thin veil of gasses banding the earth

•

Dreams change.
>   I was cutting my steak when I thought
the fantasies of the great public create the President or King
meanwhile as he sits on his throne they run their eyes over him
the way you study a roast before slicing it

they take him apart chew until he is human
now everyone is immortal has a sacred tiny place inside that can't die

Dreams change. Women kill their mothers & won't confess
and the secret men keep is a fake, nothing, meaningless

the city falling out of the cunt
the city fountaining from the cock
making caves sleeping in them

one second out of the womb with a hard-on
everyone asleep inside
everyone in Philadelphia on the edge of sleep building another Philadelphia

                •

my 5 holy cities are

                    where my grandfather died
                    where I fell in love first
                    where the lights failed
                    where I met the woman I live with
                    where

I'm telling you the lowest and by far the largest layer of
incorporated experience is physio-chemical and has no psychic
representation whatsoever except in

THE MINER'S DESK

One time there was a prince.
He loved girls.
One time when he was walking out in the forest

he saw some colors behind a tree.
And then he saw a lady.
He was very happy.
He asked the lady "Would you marry me?"
Well, if I were you, I would say "No."
If I were you I would know that you're nice.
Then the prince went on without the princess.
Then the King saw a giant monster.
The giant monster said "Here's my paw!"
"What do you think of my paw?"
"Tragedy, that's tragedy. You got a thumb in there!"
But the King just went off.
The giant's name was Billy The Manager.
So, well, in time he got married,
and he got a baby.
A boy and a girl and a kitten.
The moral is
You never go off in the forest when there is ladies
who do not know to change their minds to marry.

•

The truth of the spirit is it should fall
Frank turning to stone, feet
Charlie eating 3000 girls, lumps
Jeff burying himself in a wolf, back
Nick thrown up on the clouds of green wood, kidneys
Millie shaking the blue wave, belly
Bill cooking his elbow, bladder
Steve owning himself, lungs

Open thy mouth for the dumb in the cause of all such as are appointed
to destruction

in one dream
the door between rooms was a glass wall covered with blood

•

Killing is a form of our wandering sorrow
what parents do with their love

three year old abducted and found near death among the gravestones in
    Oak Lane

a man sitting alone late at night drunk in front of the TV
unrolls his socks
by themselves his hands move against each other
his wife sleeps his dog sleeps
he remembers himself in a hotel room the night his mother died
hands clutching the windowsill
he remembers the small river loaded with coaldust in upstate Pennsyl-
    vania
he thinks of his eyes
of his heart
of his insides falling apart

                              "It's hell to think you only have about 10 years
                                    left!!"
3000 dollars for new teeth at 61

you look young tonight
touch it keep touching it
it's good isn't it
Oh put it in God you're wonderful!

There's a moment like a strong man's cry of pain
between the abysses of being that chew on themselves

in which God shows love and the body feels
His delicate hand like a weight

Until then we have suffered so much silence
we have looked everywhere like blind men so often
we have been smeared with so much horror and emptiness
that between shadows His presence burns

●

Each image each vision each dream each word each
unfathomable part of his own living flesh is someone else
gods, bending through the darkness over a loved face
no light but yours from the light inside your mouths
other houses in the distance
                              the interrupting stars
heaven pasted on the ceiling of my daughters' room
and a moon and the sun

god who eats as we do

      I was in a loaf of bread and a German cut it into little bits and
         saw me
      I flew away I had wings on me
      I was in a kettle and drank up all the water Mother could not
         find me
      I went under the gas pipes
      The first man in the world makes clouds like small children
         on both sides of his body

as we do

●

Germantown, June 1970, through binoculars Brownlee watches a girl
walk by under his window
his prick tingles hand holds the glasses hand reaches down
still watching as she turns a corner a last snatch of leg
his eyes close the binoculars still held up
Oedipus magnifying a black nothing
wonk wonk wonk he comes on his knee and sags back

see two snakes fucking & you get tits like Tiresias

and in the center of Philadelphia the immortal flesh of the skycrapers
   rises
and wives? what are the wives doing

> there's a tiny etching of Gray's
> Ferry in Watson's Annals of Phila-
> delphia, a delicate wavy bridge
> across the Schuylkill, which is
> gone & the whales gone and

"I have formerly seen aged persons
not possessing more than ordinary
knowledge of plants for family medicines
who could tell me in a walk through the woods
or fields the medicinal uses of
almost every shrub or weed we passed . . ."

> Jamestown weed for asthma
> pokeberries as a plaster for cancer
> sour dock root as an ointment for the
>   itch
> burdock leaves on the feet to reduce
>   fever
> mullein steaming for the bowels
> motherwort in childbirth cases
> catmint tea for colic
> blackberry roots for dysentery

the inner bark of the oak and of the wild cherry tree sassafras roots
   and flowers to purify and thin the blood
put your feet in water with beech leaves
grape-vine will make your hair grow
magnolia to produce sweat
mix it with hog lard for sores
bayberry for toothache
cedar-tree berries if you have a weak spine

The Indians said they regarded the whole kingdom of vegetation as
   appointed for "the healing of nations"

127

and the first and third volumes of Watson's Annals destroyed by my
    children, or lost,
drawn on, made into paper planes, burnt, pictures cut out, hidden,
    thrown in fights,
you name it. As usual only the middle volume is left, a lone belly with-
    out head or legs.

                        •

In this city between two rivers the anxiety of stone and glass, money
    and fat,
smoke, humidity, warfare of the wild bare glance of the stranger with
    too much
human stink in his head, teeth grinding to a powder the phantoms of
    the other,
but alone
                the young wait and smoke and concentrate on the body
                soft wisps of hair under the armpits between legs
                child lost to you given to you yours
                leaves tossing the true breath of their lives outward outward
                static the human

                        •

Like the shiny unseen greasy braid on a Chinaman's head, my brain
    "If only someone could let them all go,
    let them scatter anywhere, each on the way he chose,
    so that everyone would be free to follow his own desires
    like me on this day at this hour!"

locked together in the posture of man & wife
like dragons coil on coil

                        •

a man staggers down to the base of Popo
nameless yellow flowers clumped everywhere on the snow's edge
beehives spaced out in rows just below us
beautiful days of the mother
with a five-hundred mile gaze

•

a child's finger traces the hairs on my arms
happy about the wonder of the flesh
but this isn't the history of the West the foundation of being with each
  other
instead
            bodies are torn apart quiz program reign the whisper of break-
            fast cereals
is the voice of God instead the newscasters weep before and after each
  program
the viewers dry up are found sitting next to a beer can in the morning
  like husks
instead the toilet sucks its chest in and declaims
the jetstream recites its ethical program for the future of mankind
the steamers crawl into the sad open light of the next cargo and the
decks almost go under as we worship heaviness instead
the airconditioner hums its lovesongs to the wall fire escapes give their
black sparkling bones their pathways to the sun the sun fades
the radiator gurgles its tinny hello the fat violent drivers
step on the gas hoping you'll be passing there when the brakes fail
the courts fill the hearts fill the hands fill the ears fill the
lungs fill the stomachs fill the cunts fill the nostrils fill the dogs fill
and the cats and the roofs fill with something unseen but important
the windows fill the chimneys fill the steps fill the stores fill the holes
in the moon fill the sewers fill the words fill the glasses fill the spoons
  fill
the sinks fill the chairs fill the pores fill even the invisible souls fill
and the lips
each one on each body on the earth fill

            •

Did my hand ever touch your hair?
Did my fingers ever feel your soft hair?
My heavy shoes are not as warm as the body of my wife
a horse farts
4 or 5 suffer on the ferry
you break your ass for money
when you're afraid of your wife

three white hairs in my sideburn,
my daughter pees
in the toilet with the door open and reads from a book to me,
my grandmother on her deathbed whispering "If I could only go home,"

Superman cards, Gargantua, the world's most terrifying creature,
strange photographs of a Jewish English teacher in his classroom
    blurry-headed
printed twice with huge white borders
twins talking literature puppets visionaries epiphanic dumbassed nut
sincere dope poet husband of the poet with only 8 decent words to say

and nothing comes back
but a halo
presented to the "complete man" by his tribe,
who has not lost the "first spirit"

                    •

"Your milk is sour!" as I wake and smell it flop out of my mouth
strange illuminated miracle of the world with a breast gone

"dark lords who wait until the children exhaust themselves"

How can the spirit of the earth like the white man?
everywhere the white man has touched it it is sore

                    •

What's it about?
                The little hut falls down.
                Tomorrow, debts.
                I always compare you to a drifting log with iron nails
                    in it.
                I always compare you, my mother, to the sun passing
                    behind clouds.

DARK LORDS

                some words darken the light
                and some have the teeth of rats in them
                some cannot reply

some do nothing but pray
some demand by waiting for you to give
some do nothing but command
some are really not there, tentative unreal flutters of
   the neck sending out fragments muted killings re-
   sentments
some are a needle weaving gray wool in and out of
   what you say
some are meant for silence voices that listen or bathe
some move across your chest like a rake
some question some answer some do both ask you to
   do both

•

Near the end of his life dying of tuberculosis Chekhov lay in the hospital
Tolstoi visited him with an idea, argued
writing is great only if an uneducated peasant understands it
Chekhov relapsed seriously after the great man walked out in a rage

sandpaper the soles of your feet so you can walk on anything without
   pain
You were a stranger to sorrow: thus Fate has cursed you
I am nothing. Speak of me as nothing. The dead are nothing in the
breathless dark, sunless houses, the black god

                         "Images of disaster crush us
                              all."

But I say God's face is like the doorknob on my bathroom door, shiny
   with a hole in it
I say God's face is the color of the veins in the yellow petal
I say the city of God is tear-shaped built by the soft emptying of the
   angel of grief
I say God's face is spattered with the wet leaves a storm rips off
I say God's face does not stop to look or judge or be complimented
God's face is a marble-shooting contest between the sons and daugh-
   ters of the Mayor
and the sons of the poor black starvation experts on my block
I say God's face is the first cut a child gets on his finger and screams at
I say God's face is the shopping list with candy and celery forgotten
God's face swims in your face afterimage of flashbulbs and moons

I say God's face is a stain on a torn windowshade in a house you hate to
see
I say God's face is excluded from handball pool wiretapping chess
God's face laps water like a dog on a sweltering day in the first city
I say God's face ours God's face whines God's face rests in hope buck-
les and creaks
God's face wiggles its long extended flashing dance in the wires
not in the eye not in the lips not in the ear not in the nostrils or the hand
I say God's face is always the King thrown up on a branch by 5 madmen
the immoral female dancers going wild stamping down roots Pentheus
Judas in the tree
cities in the hushed rhythms of their feet in the bleeding grass cities
where death smiles endlessly out of the known face on you you love
sown in dishonor raised in glory sown in weakness raised in power

and as we have borne the image of the earthy
we shall also bear the image of the heavenly
we shall not all sleep
but we shall all be changed
                              on 7th Street between Lombard & Pine
vision of the wheel sofas draped with oilcloth heaven of the black
of the flickering blue tubes of images playing on the bodies of the
dancers
kitchen chair thrones crown jewels in a cigar box the dead light
of standards and commodities is the light of heaven
God tastes the sweet savor of Christ here death tastes life life tastes
death

for God loves a cheerful giver rude in speech but not in knowledge

and on 7th & Lombard in the corner bar everyone says "Fuck You!"
until his tongue falls out and he throws himself against
some other black drunken unhealed healer without faith
back into the first arms he knew Mother Fucker into the arms
the funny rages of the deaths we rehearse for them
                                    the white man's eye

sees his own soul secret intestinal knot
his own eaten-out life shining in the black sweating churches of the
    unsaved

WHO WAIT

•

the statue of William Penn crowning City Hall
whatever side you look at it from
looks like the scroll in his hand is a cock

my fantasy is he had a Rabbi for a father and a black mother
who scrubbed the long marble halls until her death
her kneecaps were permanently locked so she could kneel but not stand

•

I saw one of the beasts heads
it was wounded to death
but the deadly wound was healed
everyone wondered at it

they worshipped the beast saying
who is like him? who can battle him?
and he was given a mouth
and the power to speak for 42 months

and he could make war with the saints
and beat them

and the Beast crucified the Son of God afresh

•

These days on everything
windshields revolving doors forearms
the American flag waves its stiff wave

cyanide in a hollow cap on his tooth, Himmler bit down

      from *The Book Of Masters:*
"The official language of government is reason, and only reason.
It's a new form of paranoia: fear of the unconscious, unconscious
fear of death. But their actions are irrational. You combat this
with irrational speech, and in these times only comic paranoid fantasies,
stabs at why these maniacs act as they do, can uncover the meaning
of the sickness of power politics. 'I don't trust a man unless I
have his pecker in my pocket' means I can't die if I castrate you.
When you are faced with an incredibly mad, destructive reality
you can explain it only by a free exploration of motives through fantasy
and alogical insight."

•

Revelation Inc., a new company, non-profit, nothing but a room with
    telephones
and the workers calling everyone in the phonebook once a day for a year
one office in each city over 50,000
"Hello, Bill, you're dying . . ." "Hello, Frank, you're dying . . ." "Hello,
    Jane,
you're dying . . ." until everyone's heard it 365 times and can't escape
cruel mad funny ridiculous impossible sick dumb meaningless?

UNTIL

the body is formed
the I drinks the I

134

until it falls back withers and dies

THE CHILDREN

kids joke about the body especially its dark shitty holes
song of the Tootsie Roll and the goldfish of the nipple and the
belly tingle the tongue licking its toys

Jeff showed me this
                    "Whose is it then,
                    my children,
                    this red, red moon?"

Isaa's mother died when he was three
making him the only passionate Haiku poet
syllables that made all months the Hunger Month for him
emptiness of the moon in water
trembling milky disc men think of when

not like our Presidents and Kings who put death somewhere else
in the faces of the poor Asian in the babyshit of the African
in the delicate huts of people who grow things and are always praying
on TV and know they die

                •

Synagogue, temple I left after I made my thirteen year old speech
    against murder,
I keep thinking I'll go back
smelling the flame, sneezing from the old crumbling prayer books,
to the erratic torn voice of the cantor
ripping the heart out until it praises
joy in the marrow joy in the cells joy in the structural unknown miracle
    of the first spirit
nothing city of the commandments of

135

at the center of the first cities graveyards and temples stood
men sang out the holy syllables & nothing else

and the poet's work on the white paper is
blind fishgod crawling up onto the edge of the Oedipal mind gasping
    transformed
city on the lips in the beginning

●

The city lies between two rivers
like the head of a man on his wife's breasts

the city you wake from, enter, sleep against, beg for its light and buy
and the city is the wound of the self called Joseph, Bill or Susan
what are we who master everything?
King & Queen, the zero, the unreal treasure

just as the oyster heals its wound with a pearl
the god is the place that heals

●

go nowhere listen to yourself

boats glide past on the river below Front Street
maybe   maybe

all these houses beneath the waters beneath the earth beneath and
    above
in all forms filled with crying and with the laughter of children

Why did we lift up the word?
what good was love?
which wall
held back death? where was
the black child who guarded you?

●

because
because they threw gloves on the box
because of that
it stutters under the neck like a chicken because it's a man
because whips cut unfinished white circles over the listener's head
because you say so little about it when they ask
beat the door in agony
yes to everything you've said and no
underneath to the fear because you said nothing useful
ten million babies framed in steel
fossils deep in the walls where you eat and talk about it
fists crumbling teeth fighting out of their sockets
the doctor looking into her closed eyes
his eyes dripping
all because not one arrived on time for the other
the doors lifted onto their hinges
the half face burning downstairs like a lamp
the head reading and sinking into the pages
the cheeks wrinkling like water
the wounds curling
because
because you

tiny lights that the eyes reach out for
fringe the sky
distances cool between two skins
then the moon
lost forever where it lets its flat useless
light cover the floor

●

a dragon singing in a withered tree
the pupils of the eyes of a skull
filled with joy
is there anyone who can hear the dragon singing?
everyone does
what was this eye
a toad dancing up to heaven?
like a flake of snow in a redhot fire
misleading   I
touch whatever is left
father your strangled prayers float to the ceiling
of the temple in my dream
smoke
Oh those eyes!
yours blinded with tears His invisible

●

In all the dark stretches of the Atlantic down from the hills of North
    Philly
a black water accumulates   what are we?

in the shadows of his curtains and in the folds of his silent pillows
are not these the places of religion?
                              EXHAUST THEMSELVES

FIVE

THE QUEEN'S TRIANGLE

A romance

Ted ate her.

His mother teeters on a window sill.
Bill hears someone scream.
Mr. K. is burying sausage in the back yard.
The girl slips away into a wall.

Ted stumbles up to the bathroom mirror.

The air falls and is trapped.
No more voices.
The old man without teeth curses.
A scratching somewhere behind the wall.

Ted washes and feels scared.

When we hear about it a fist inside squeezes.
The world is a 'they'.
One eyelid begins twitching.
Underneath suddenly fills and we go deeper.

Ted sits down and thinks.

I am sitting on a red cushion in my room.
I did it and fear myself.
I want to sleep but the wind begs me.
I feel the worst questions again.

Ted begins sweating and peels off his shirt.

Bill and I live in different parts of the city.
He likes hunting.
I like darts.
Mine is my father and his is his mother.

Ted feels everything looks strange.

Mr. K.'s windows advertise medicine.
Mrs. K. dreams about haircuts.
Bill hunts animals in order to empty his rifle.
I know he wants a useless gun for the big kill.

Ted misses her.

Outside some of the grass is withering.
The sun and the moon give exactly the same light.
Whatever war is fought is silent.
The five of us curse a murderous family.

Now Ted knows about the bad twin.

Bill's mother opens me up.
Mouths come after me.
A dark tear fills Bill's head.
Mr. K. drinks and laughs through nine teeth.

Ted watches us across the Canadian border.

The past is a wing without feathers.
Mrs. K. unhooks her brassiere and cries.
O the sagging we are as we fuck and pray.
Bill is beginning to make his own bullets.

Ted's left arm floats over Philadelphia.

My wife dreams of the resurrection of pure love.
I sit on my ass perfectly at one with my ass.
Bill becomes the great American poet of toe cheese.
Mr. and Mrs. K. lie in bed thinking about it.

Ted's tongue has fallen into it again.

Something flies down on hot nights to take us.
Let it come get it over with I can't wait.
I don't want to go but I have gone and go.
The whole family has opened up with Not Enough!

Ted hears the careless moaning of angels.

Bill sneaks upstairs and looks in a drawer.
I look in the refrigerator but nothing's there.
The old lady stares out the window.
The old man laughs over invisible sausages.

Ted gnaws a hole through the bedroom wall.

Police from the closest star glide down.
Everyone is naked.
Everyone dances on the edge and falls.
Everyone is being followed and locked up.

Ted is empty.

Bill flies back to the house on the river.
Mrs. K. tries to remember what it was like.
It was like surgery for metaphysical purposes.
Mr. K. remembers how silence cures the lost wounds.

Ted takes up golf with stolen clubs.

On the St. Lawrence a rowboat has gone down.
The newspapers say the passengers are unknown.
I buy groceries for the week.
Bill drives North only to come back stunned.

Isn't Ted ready?

This belt and that sock don't match.
Bill counts the cables on the Walt Whitman Bridge.
I go crazy on the railroad trestle over the Chesapeake.
A big someone has faith and lies back and goes beyond words.

Ted can't bring his legs through the wall.

Bill's mother sighs in the lonely darkness.
She looks at her hand and a small fire bursts in it.
Mr. K. in the garden drops to his knees secretly.
Bill gropes for the trigger as I grope for the face.

Ted is writing a letter.

Imagine it says More More More Yes No.
Dream about its first image of roots and breasts.
Hope it concludes with a sentence on holy despair.
Expect so much of it you want to die when it comes.

Ted says little.

It rained today and we walked through a slum.
We ate dinner at a good place.
When we got home we thought about all of you.
Nothing happens so what can I say except Love.

Ted hangs Gauguin's Christ on the bathroom wall.

In his classrooms Bill reaches out.
A sharp pain splinters his mother's chest.
Mr. K. reads the news and calls out NO!
I am talking to a famous baby elephant in the zoo.

Ted hopes again as he tastes the nipple.

But we know.
Nothing reverses the plot.
Sometimes you think a bird's jagged song will do it.
But it does what it does to you.

Ted listens to a religious voice.

Who has given more to see God than I have?
Who has believed and yelled *You*
Who needs it with as much pain?
Whose guilt fills as many bathroom sinks as mine?

Ted wipes his lips.

The moon lets a milky scum of light paint the clubs.
Their heads gleam slightly like skulls.
Maybe they belong to men from another planet.
Bill thinks they look like iron flowers.

Ted holds her hand.

I have decided on insects.
Mrs. K. touches her husband's thigh softly.
Mr. K. belches as he leans back.
Bill flies down between them as chicken hawk.

Ted crouches in the woods waiting for him.

O he isn't there because both of you aren't.
Bill draws one of his Polish surreal landscapes.
I get a letter suggesting I'm a dumb faggot.
Mr. K. smokes his third pack and pours another.

Ted is planting window boxes again.

All I ever said was I Understand Yes I know OK.
Nevertheless the story goes on as usual.
Birds dive and land on the same branches.
Many cry and the others have no destiny.

Ted's left testicle aches.

But it's clear now the family is blue.
Everyone fucking and strangling without sleep.
The Mrs. looks sad as she lifts the toilet seat.
Everything spirals for the last time.

Ted prays under a stranger's window.

God's weird quiet language spills over us like milk.
Bill kisses his father O the terrible breathing.
And I take five aspirin knowing they won't help.
All that helps is keeping it in as long as possible.

Ted knows this is true.

The sausage is ready under a foot of earth.
Dragonflies raid the windows where she knits.
I break in through the second floor window.
Feet hushed with towels wrapped over my shoes.

Ted sleeps late.

The dream all of us have is breaking his teeth.
In the middle of the night I get up doubled.
Something like acid has dripped into my mouth.
Mr. K. speaks for the first time in twelve years.

Ted squeezes a pimple.

On a road we haven't built unraised bodies stay down.
Each form is naked preparing to lie.
Names and clouds coming down in a blanket.
I look for the one who twisted my bicycle.

Ted gnaws his fingers.

You should have seen the Mrs. wiggling her ass.
I could barely eat my fruit cocktail.
The Sausage King sipped his bourbon.
Bill couldn't believe it was them not him.

Ted squeezes his temples and can't speak.

She heard this and threw dark threads over the trembling river.
Dreamer of furious oceans cold sleeper of weeds and shells.
Of course Bill and Steve don't believe this.
We survive by touching as little as possible.

Ted begins breaking things.

A glass winks at him from five places.
Shoe laces and pants in the air.
Dollars out the window into my awed hands.
Blood breaking out in a few pinpricks on the neck.

Ted picks an onion from the bowl.

It crinkles and has a sad abysmal look to it.
I replace it with a stroke from behind.
Bill nuzzles a slice before kissing her.
Mr. K. chews the first sausage that's ready on Sunday.

Ted forces her to bite into it.

Was it laughter that broke at the peak decibel?
Are we engaged in the immortal clash of guns?
She can't stop gobbling it and shakes apart.
That old distant eye looks down as it always will.

Ted sees all three doing nothing.

He can't find Bill's hand in the raging twilight.
His head and the red sun slip into each other.
Fathers pray for the resurrection of fathers.
Mothers wail for the children of the false void.

Ted can't get up.

Teeth and claws are hooked into the windowsill.
Something climbs in like a slave wordless through power.
The man triples himself and rips it all.
No one sees the death his death tiptoes inside.

Ted has only hands left.

Mrs. K. undresses in front of the mirror silently.
Mr. K. watches with such sadness I could cry.
Bill crawls in and looks up at the gods parading.
I hide in the closet all ears and one hand working.

Ted says the end.

But the holy noises return meaning Harma Sen Roo Nickrod.
Dr. God greatest of experts loses the patient.
Bill jumps from the chair and tears things.
I watch and grow afraid of what's next.

Ted drives back to be captured.

The outer police and the inner guards have joined forces.
They find him on the top shelf of his bedroom closet.
I put my secret guerrillas into operation.
Soon the three groups will fight for the one.

Ted waits in her hands.

Bill cleans his shotgun and loads it.
I send messages to each member of the star navy.
No reply.
Mr. K. harvests his crop and stares.

Ted is amazed he can walk.

Two red holes sprout on the dreamer's belly.
The K.s swim in a circle through the attackers.
Coral blooms on their lips.
The sky fills with ack-ack in a favorite movie.

Ted kneels.

Bill manages to unsheath the knife and cut himself.
The tip bleeds a lot.
Mrs. K. pours boiling water on her hand.
Whose sleep turns itself out into the light?

Ted is lifted by The Real Hands.

His missing tooth grows back in carved gold.
The Master of the K.s envies it and wants ten.
I dream that the last Bible is grafted onto her thigh.
Each line of each page is reduced to an ash.

Ted drinks three glasses before retiring.

Someone studies the evolution of trilobites.
One sees his hand as a fossil that strangers x-ray.
Another goes mad at ten thousand feet looking for bones.
Mrs. K. notices eight new wrinkles on her leg.

Ted can't.

In a room hidden from us under the city he sits in a chair.
Wires are taped to his eyelids and flow from a transformer.
When they plug it in his screams reach the neighborhood.
Hands in the middle of eating hang there lips freeze.

Ted sees his wife after death.

We inherit the virtues of the Polypterus.
The guards change uniforms and resemble old friends.
The heat melts their cosmetic noses as they grin.
The Pain Is Freedom sign over the exit keeps us calm.

Ted passes into a new realm.

Mrs. K. is feeding ten thousand infants from a single breast.
Mr. K. is the last.
A cloud reddens over my shoulder and swaddles the bones.
The snake protects its eggs in a dry coil.

Ted relaxes.

The heaven bells ring like an axe in a planetary skull.
The ships circle West and dive and threaten us.
Mrs. K. irons an old housedress with green flowers on the hem.
Mr. K. trips on a shovel.

Ted sees his mother's face become a black wheel.

Ted's hands are like rhubarb now.
His wife is flown in for questioning.
His mother ties red strings on all the doorknobs.
His father keeps trying to drink walls stones cactus cars.

Ted confesses.

No faces guide the star navy's first attack.
Suddenly children stop the word game.
Toys begin speaking giving wild orders break.
A new tranquilizer becomes the key to celestial mechanics.

Ted bites his knuckles.

The action of the small intestine wrecks the heart.
Mrs. K. is institutionalized in a bust of white soap.
Mr. K. worships at the altar of the lost message.
I get up at 9 and see myself at the funeral of grass.

Ted calls himself General.

The great smile under the braids and ribbons lasts for years.
The tanks have Ted's face painted on them.
Mrs. K. calls her husband in for a ham frozen dinner.
The TV has an infinite store of second images.

Ted signs himself Hazy Universe.

Mr. K. organizes the neighborhood and teaches sleepwalking.
The nation arms for the attack of poor saints and bees.
The President calls in Bill for advice.
He says the whites of their eyes are painted.

Ted's drugstore closes.

The druggist has taken an overdose.
He is found on a toothpaste rack next to the mint flavors.
The candy stand melts.
The sunglasses stare into a depopulated infinity.

Ted takes over.

Bill works at the toy counter selling lethal balloons.
Mrs. K. gives free haircuts to lesbians.
Sampes of the star navy's kills are stacked like newspapers.
Little pieces of the night accumulate unnoticed.

Ted addresses the people.

Have faith in the frail hairy caves of the moon.
Let your hands wrinkle a salesman's face.
Empty your pockets into the brown river of steel reeds.
Give your mouths to the white zero.

Ted is impeached.

Mrs. K. can't understand why her boy failed.
Mr. K. dozes on the roof of his red Chevrolet.
Bill comes home only to find weaknesses enshrined.
For six hours he bites his pillow.

Ted buys a ticket to Peoria.

The landscape blurs in the sallow moonlight.
This torpedo of seated people going nowhere cuts through.
A few words between the passengers when it hurts.
A cheese sandwich on an old magazine in a bag on a lap.

Ted arrives.

In the house where scarcheek the nurse waits Ted finds love.
The baby is drained off and burned.
The galaxy of bright anchors changes location.
Lenses in the biggest telescopes crumble mysteriously.

Ted wipes his face.

The K.s are meeting to decide one another's fate.
On the radio a watery troubled voice gives orders.
Something about shelter keeping inside taking stock.
People feel a mild burning sensation along the hairline.

Ted's golden city collapses.

But the celluloid elephant stampedes to his doorstep.
Claws rake across left and right.
Mud bears the soft letters of the God.
Bill hoes through the brains of worms in a Victory Garden.

Ted is seen lecturing.

In order to recognize what it is we beg sleep.
In order to talk about it we wear ties.
In order to slip it in we grow tired.
In order to reason well we get very angry.

Ted is promoted.

Bill keeps a midget angel locked in a shirt drawer.
Even at this hour it struggles.
Its wings visit the sleep of the butcher.
Its song is a flake of tinfoil on a silver tooth.

Ted wakes the eel.

At the family dinner what is eaten fights back.
The Mrs. takes her teeth out and whistles.
The floor calls for lighter feet.
Mr. K. washes it down with a big gulp of guinea red.

Ted whispers to God.

All this time the fears have been deepening their nest.
O the beaks swallow the air.
The claws gripping what fits like drops of water.
One arm against a country of arrows.

Ted hears the word.

Bill refuses to talk in class today.
The students shift and mumble to each other.
He thinks The Big Finger is branding his head.
But one says the questions are silly and answers.

Ted's mission is clear.

In a suit made of tan cotton K. drives through the night.
The trees blacken at his side.
The distances are so great he is a gnat in them.
Tiny houselights twinkle and fade in the cold woods.

Ted buys a long wool robe with a hood.

At the gates to the Water City his cup fills.
One building casts a shadow that doesn't change.
There is a hand shaping this as it strikes down.
The leaves of the pickle bush are ragged and thin.

Ted can't understand death.

In Ted's sleep the refrigerator becomes President again.
War is declared between the roofs and pavements.
The end of anything panics the spine.
Thrones decay in the belly of the Texas ruler.

Ted forgets how to walk.

In the middle of her sleep Mrs. K. goes downstairs for a snack.
Mr. K. turns to the empty side of the bed and embraces it.
Bill sneaks upstairs as the first escaped prisoner.
The agony of the sun gets no sympathy.

Ted finds the mountain.

He tears off a sleeve and makes a flag and plants it on top.
After two weeks of meditation he learns three new words.
A week later he forgets them.
Pieces of his skin stick between each one.

Ted remembers.

It was the way she tore it out of my mouth.
It was the early dreams of losing it.
It was how she held me and told the exterminator where to spray.
It was the cosmic birthday of two sad faces.

Ted steals matches from her pocketbook.

The little bull terrier is having its back legs torn apart.
Mrs. K. screams with fear gathers a dust cloud.
It is a beautiful summer afternoon in the third city.
Baseball is popular among the middle class boys.

Ted's hobby is solid models.

From one corner of the sky a formation crawls in.
We hear about surrender half-assed reports of the flash.
Twenty-five years later we still dream about mile-long scars.
Mrs. K.'s mouth drops open in sleep and fills with pink ashes.

Ted smiles.

Dinner at the K.s with polka music and home brew.
The Wildcat and P-38 float on threads from a bedroom ceiling.
They twirl very slowly nose downwards.
Bill hears the wing guns open up between explanations.

Ted sands the Zero's fuselage.

Bill's face is yellow and slit-eyed in the cockpit.
Somewhere in the boy's mind enemy fighters take the air.
Each one is flown by a paper replica of The Mr. & Mrs.
The Zero has twenty-nine American stars painted on its side.

Ted sets fire to a pile of shavings.

It's humid under the stairs where the girls do it.
I crawl under and see everyone half undressed O Dr. Dr. it's here!
Bicycles piled up everywhere chained to the storage bins.
I completely forget what I saw.

Ted eats a ham sandwich.

The bad twin finds the good twin at the next desk in school.
The good twin finds a bad one that does anything.
Bill visits the girl who blows over the telephone.
Mr. K. has an image of a sixteen-year-old honey blonde.

Ted reads a book about the body of love.

Mrs. K. sees her three best friends strangled.
But the dream overlaps and she keeps her hands tied all day.
Mr. K. laughs and dances drunk in his underpants.
The neighbors see him in the back yard a flabby ghost.

Ted cures himself of the clap.

At the dirty book store Bill and I are at home.
I tell him about my father's silk Chinese picture book.
38 positions in full color detailed.
We imagine how Blake saw priests and nuns boffing like mad.

Ted faces the screen.

Only a vague dark face hovers on the other side listening.
The sins of men are forgiven by the bloodless.
The obscure one fiddles with himself his cross jangles.
The true Christ works up a sweat playing tennis.

Ted feels lighter.

Dr. Crucified reveals himself.
A big hook nose a moustache very Jewish believe me.
The armpits of the real J.C. are thick and shaggy.
Whoever drinks from his mouth laughs his balls off knows all serves
    hard.

Ted converts to the Church of the One-Armed Bandit.

The Queen appears for split seconds.
She flashes on both sides and is never recognized.
But even her absence is magnetic.
So many pray after a look at what might have been her smile.

Ted says nothing.

On the Pentagon steps five baby hands have been left by a strange god.
Each one is filled with quivering ashes.
Mrs. K. plants gladiolas against her basement windows.
Bill digs up half an acre with a kitchen knife.

Ted sees himself broken by love.

Something about the spool at the end of a kitestring calls me.
Mr. K. stares into his hand.
The corn is fierce in slow motion.
It's sadder looking down into the floppy lettuce leaves.

Ted crawls into the night.

Who am I looking for when I take those long evening walks?
Such a little voice comes from the river.
It doesn't cure the sitting up straight or the clean spoons.
Even Bill's magic markers are drained by the orders.

Ted is being lifted up.

Images of a life rise in my chest like drowning suddenly.
Bill breaks his leg painting Mr. K.'s roof.
Mrs. K. freezes multicolored beetles in ice cubes.
At the annual blast she puts them on show around the roast beef.

Ted hangs there.

Children break in time after time to remind us.
On a mild Friday afternoon Bill finds himself paralyzed.
Mrs. K. is decorating the Sun Ray Drug windows.
Mr. K. darns like a spider under the bathroom sink.

Ted looks down.

Bill's eyes stare into the last radiance man will see.
I move my hands crisply over something I almost recognize.
It speaks and the vision of pity's female ace blinds me.
Mrs. K. is obsessed with the time between the street and window.

Ted is white as a cabbage heart.

Behind the dining room table a mirror traps all of us.
Bill sweats from the boiled potatoes.
The Mr. & Mrs. eat slowly while their thoughts curdle.
I want nothing more than the crude response of a dog.

Ted.

Ted winks.

The King.
Billy The Manager.
The Queen.
The Prince.

Ted defines tragedy.

At the usual Sunday dinner the family is blinded.
Bill knows it's just to get laid or get rich.
Money weeps in the pockets of the sexless.
Sex dries in the mouths of the poor like husks.

Ted realizes and wakes.

The fighters have broken away from their threads.
The dinner is ruined by a new attack.
The planes carry pennies under their wings.
Everyone is a piggy bank with a slit in his head.

Ted returns to America.

Mom and Dad are crying on fresh hosed steps odor of stone?
The Welcome Banner limps in the twilight breeze.
Now the houses are empty the pets curl up the lights cool.
Bill stiffens at the head of the fire parade.

Ted thanks everyone for the medals.

Mrs. K. takes up reading the great poets through a mask.
Mr. K. changes his underpants once a week.
Bill has as many women as the King of Arabia's favorite steed.
I hang up my clothes as usual and kiss them tango act dumb.

Ted is lifted down and covered.